THE JEWS OF GREECE

An Essay
by Nicholas Stavroulakis

Talos Press

ISBN No. 960-7459-00-8

Published in Greece by Talos Press
Kifisias 10
115 26 Athens
Greece
Tel: 771-0417

Typeset in Greece by Fotron S.A.
Printed in Greece

Cover: Menorah carved on marble found in the Ancient Agora of Athens, 500 C.E.

In memory of Alfredos Mordoh

THE JEWS OF GREECE: *An Essay*.

by *Nicholas Stavroulakis*

Modern Greek Jewry is a minor, if not insignificant, community in the Diaspora, numbering approximately 5,000 persons, most of them citizens of Greece, speaking Greek, and in one way or another influenced by their Greek identity. It is difficult today to imagine a world—that of Late Antiquity—when out of the ten million inhabitants of the Roman Empire, some one million were Jews: the vast majority of whom lived in cities that had been founded by Alexander the Great or his successors, or built according to Greek urban ideals by the Romans. This was a world of intense internationalism; and, while Latin may have been the language of government and law, Greek was the lingua franca of this urbanism that stretched from Spain to Mesopotamia. It was within this Greek-speaking and, hence Greek-thinking, world that Jews were forced to re-examine their identity as a people among the nations. And, it was into this world that Jews immigrated to find a haven after the fall of the 2nd Temple in 71 C.E. and the even greater disaster following the Bar Kochba Revolt. Ironically, it was within this world that modern post-Exilic and Rabbinic Judaism was born, as was its estranged sister, Christianity.

Despite our romanticism in the 20th century, the ideals of this world have all but vanished. Nationalism—a revival or re-assertion of tribalism—has been built on the ruins of this world of antiquity, the fragments of which are incongruously incorporated in our thoughts, institutions and aspirations. Identities, national and racial, have been built and ordered by modern romantic revisionism. The descendants of the very people who destroyed the ancient world dig assiduously in its ruins to find some link with the past,

5

some sense of identity with it. Modernism, or at best a humanism lacking in any definition of humanity, has replaced Christianity. The values that we once took for granted in government have been overthrown by the modern state and its politicians. Ours is a world of violent and rapid change; it is no surprise that we seek roots, some point of reference whereby to order our identity. This may, of course, simply be the way things are. Change being the very nature of existence and resistance to it being one of the signs of our humanity--whichever the case may be—the Jews of Greece have survived some 2,300 years of change and are a living link with antiquity.

Of all the peoples living in modern Greece it is perhaps the Jews who know their *Greekness*, in the historical sense, most immediately. Foreign occupation, wars, invasions and conversion, have alienated the modern Christian Greek from the the historic and tangible realities of Classical Antiquity. The gouged crosses still to be seen in the ruins of Eleusis, the imposition of churches on the ruined foundations of shattered temples are stern reminders to any romantic of the violent and sharp break that occurred with the religion and values of pagan antiquity in the great age of Greece. The Greek Jew, on the other hand, faces no such contradiction when faced with the ruins of a 3rd century synagogue on the island of Delos or the mosaic of a synagogue floor on the island of Aegina. His tradition in religion, and to a great degree, the manner in which he responds to the world, are rooted in an unbroken tradition clearly traceable through the maze of Ottoman and Byzantine history, and beyond that into the age of Augustus and the birth of Jesus, to that time when, as legend describes it, Alexander the Great and the High Priest met on Mount Scopus overlooking Jerusalem.

Modern romantic and nationalistic Hellenic revivalism, rooted as it is in the secularism and pseudo-humanism of our age, has lessened the consequences of this significant divergence in perspective that the modern Greek Christian and Jew must experience in regard to the past. Both have been drawn into a new superimposed Hellenic identity that each, from a quite different perspective, must relate to. This modern *Hellenization* was strong enough to create a crisis in identity for Sephardic Jews on the eve of World War II. These descendants of Spanish and Portuguese Jews had lived an almost atrophied Iberian existence in the Ottoman Empire for 500 years. Thus, the Greek Jew has an almost Janus-like aspect to his character. On the one hand, he has an identity that is clearly Greek when placed among Jews, and, on the other, he is decidedly Jewish when he finds himself among Christian Greeks. This is, of course, undoubtedly true of many societies to a greater or lesser degree. In regard to the Greek Jew it is more pronounced due to the antiquity of his roots in Greece, and his sense of an unbroken historical continuum that marks the history of his ancestors in Greece. He is the survivor of a greater Greek-speaking world that has been shrunk to the limits of the modern Greek state.

To trace the evidence and to construct a balanced historical record of the history of the Jewish presence in Greece is beyond the scope of this essay. It should be noted, however, that such a history will never be written. The Jewish presence in Greece is not reflected well in material or documentary evidence, a problem that, interestingly, is paralleled in the study of Medieval Greece in general back into Roman times. Wars, fires, indifference, and changes in economy, have all had their effects in creating lacunae that frustrate a balanced picture of this past. There is, however, a sufficient amount of reliable material to allow us to catch a glimpse of the Jew in this vast matrix. We find him as Moschon, a Jewish slave whose name was inscribed on a tombstone of the Classic age at Oropos; we can almost grasp his visage in the encounter that Justin Martyr had in the agora of Antioch with the urbane and gentlemanly Tryphon. He is a messianic pretender who tragically attempts to lead his community by foot across the sea from Crete to Judaea in the

4th century, and others were part of the Genoese theft of Jews stolen for slavery from Modon in the 15th century. He is exiled from Spain, a Marrano who becomes himself as a Jew in Salonika; he is exiled from Greece to die in the horrors of Auschwitz. At times we are dealing with facts, at other times we are led into the richer and more bewildering realm of legend and myth, a world that perhaps reveals more than incidents circumscribed by scholar's dates.

Jewish legend, reflecting the almost magical aura surrounding the conquest of Alexander the Great, inevitably described the first encounter of Jews and Greeks in terms of a meeting between Alexander and the High Priest in Jerusalem. History, as understood by Jews was the record of God's intervention in time. Events had meanings which were in most cases moral or prophetic, and Jews could hardly ignore the incidents that led to the rise of Alexander the Great, and, correspondingly, the fall of the Persian Empire. Almost overnight the world had changed. International Hellenism forced the Jews to reassess their role among the Nations. This was the world that eventually was to see the birth of Christianity, and its sister Rabbinic Judaism.

Josephus, the Roman, Hellenized-Jewish historian and general, gives an account of this meeting. He records how Alexander, fresh from conquering the coast of Phoenicia, made his way up to Jerusalem with the intention of punishing its High Priest and destroying the City. At the time of laying seige to Tyre he had demanded of Jaddua (or Jaddus), the High Priest, provisions to feed his army. Jaddua had replied by pointing out that he was still under obligation to the Ruler of the World, Darius. He could not commit treason against his lord, and he refused to comply with the order. Alexander had vowed revenge. So that on ascending to the Holy City Alexander went to Mt. Scopus and from its summit looked down onto the Temple Mount. Once there, he and his army saw a great procession of priests and levites being led by the

8

High Priest dressed in his sacrificial robes and wearing over his forehead the diadem on which was inscribed the Tetragrammaton -(the Name of God). As the procession approached, Alexander horrified his army by suddenly throwing himself prostrate to the ground and performed *proskynesis*, (a ritual act of abasement reserved for gods, and divinely appointed kings), hardly what one performed toward a priest. When later queried by his generals, as Josephus's account goes, he revealed that before he had ever passed into Asia, when still in Macedonia, he had received a prophetic dream in which the High Priest appeared, advising him to take courage and to cross over into Asia. Alexander claimed that the figure he had seen in his dream dressed as the High Priest had been the very God of the Judaeans. Jerusalem was saved, and Alexander became part of Jewish legend.

But other legends embellish this meeting with even more extraordinary stories. It is said that Alexander sought out the Jewish scriptures and laws. He read and studied the books of Solomon and handed this literature over to his teacher Aristotle. He found references in the Book of Daniel to what he believed to be himself, regarding the overthrow of Persia. Later, when that had taken place, he took seat and assumed the power and authority of the great Shah on the Throne of Solomon. The history of this throne is interesting. Jews claimed that when the 1st Temple was destroyed, it had been carried off and was used by the kings of Babylon until Cyrus had crushed them and seized it for himself. It was from this throne that the King of Kings and Ruler of the Four Corners of the Earth ruled. It was this throne, now seized by Alexander, that was a mark of his authority as successor of the great Cyrus and Darius, and of Solomon. The great Macedonian was not only celebrated in legends such as this but was thus brought intimately into Jewish history and the great drama that it was understood to be.

The Jews were not the only peoples in the Near

East to sense the momentous changes that were taking place (or had taken place) as a consequence of Alexander's conquest. Even if one does not admit to that view of history that sees events as marked by individuals, it is hard to imagine a world without Alexander - even today. Despite Jewish legend, it is likely that Alexander, at this time, knew of neither the existence of the Jews nor of Jerusalem. If he did, it was only as one of the many minor peoples that his empire absorbed in its conquest of Persia. Great cities were to become the means of administration as well as the catalyzing loci in which oriental and Greek thought were to merge and interact. Urbanism, as defined in the *poleis* of the Classic Greeks was expanded, further developed, and embellished by Alexander and his successors. This magical, violent, romantic, and fragile, lonely man gave form to a world in which Greek and Oriental were to share and suffer the inevitable contradictions this involved. It was a period of incredible creative activity - and insecurity.

Alexander died in 321. His death threw the conquered world to the generals who had assisted him in taking it and by 270 the debris of the adjustment was settling. Egypt was in the hands of the Ptolemys who set about transorming Alexandria, the first of the cities founded by Alexander, into a centre that attracted the various peoples of the known world. Syria was ruled from Antioch by Seleucus, another general. Coele-Syria as Judaea was now called, lay between the two and was to be a bone of contention. The transformation of the rough and rugged Judaeans (not unlike the contemporary Afghanis) into an urban people was not a consequence of the influence of Jerusalem, but of the high culture of Hellenistic urbanism. Alexandria and Antioch were but two of over ninety cities that the Macedonians founded under Alexander during the great conquest of the East in the 4th century BCE.

The Greek city, in the form in which Alexander understood it, was the only place in which a man could grow and function as a person. In it he lived, fulfilled his religious obligations, and voted or filled civic offices. It was in its schools that he was educated in literature, warfare and the arts. In its markets he discussed and met the wider world. In its Classical form, however, the City of the Greeks was in a sense provincial. The constitutional model that Alexander used in founding his cities was that of Athens. According to some it was Aristotle who aided him. Athens had worked out its own laws and institutions in a situation that to a degree paralleled a problem that Jews were later to face - and perhaps never resolve - the problem of blood relationship and tribalism. In the 6th century BCE, Athens had undergone a *crisis* that had threatened its very existence.

Based on tribal relations rooted in blood ties, Athens found itself unable legally to incorporate large numbers of foreigners living within the Attic peninsula. Under great law- givers such as Solon and Cleisthenes, a means was found to undermine regional and tribal associations and to base citizenship firmly on legal associations rather than blood relationships. Still the *poleis* (city) of the Athenians was limited in its ability to think beyond its geographic limits. In the form that took under Alexander, the *poleis* became not only the administrative center of a geographically defined area but a school in which orientals were Hellenized and transformed into *Greeks*. There arose, within a very short period of time, an international urban elite made up of Macedonians, Greeks, and Hellenized Orientals who could relate easily with each other from Alexandria to Athens, and for a time, as far East as Bactria and Afghanistan. While it is true that the *poleis* was no longer a means for training men in the arts of self-determination, it did become the means of uniting the achievements of Babylon and Egypt, not to mention peripheral cultures, within a common civilization dominated by the figure of Alexander, or legends concerning his person, his ideals, and vision. The common language of its this culture was the *koine* or vulgar Greek. It has been said by the rabbis that with each language a man learns he also acquires an additional soul: the Jews of this new world inevitably were to acquire Greek souls.

The response of the Judaeans to this new world was divided. Nonetheless, it cannot be ignored in any attempt to understand either the development of Judaism or even the birth of Christianity. Ironically, despite the exciting content of the legend concerning the meeting of Alexander and the High Priest Jaddus, it does not seem that either the Jews or Jerusalem were part of this new world. Under Nehemia and Ezra in the 6th century, the returning Jews of Babylon had reconstituted a Jewish Commonwealth under Persian rule. While in Babylon they had developed institutions and means of maintaining or asserting identity that were to evolve into the synagogue and the *publication* of the Law so as to make it accessible to all. At the same time, however, the return to Judaea was also a return to tribalism, as race and blood relationships became paramount and the law of the community was that of Moses as published by Ezra. Judaism, like Hellenism, was a way of life and not simply a culture or religion. It had not, however, gone beyond the crisis that Athens had faced in the 6th century. It remained tribal and bound to its Land.

It is not surprising that we know so little about the Jewish Commonwealth. Among the nations, the Judaeans had a low if not insignificant profile. There is even a distinct possibility that this relatively silent period in Jewish history reflects stagnancy more than anything else. Was it because of this that Jews began to emigrate in great numbers to cities like Alexandria and Antioch? Already by the reign of Ptolemy Philadelphus (II), there was a large Jewish community in Egypt. Some had been slaves, still others mercenaries, certainly many must have been attracted by the riches to be made there. In 270 BCE, a translation of the Jewish scriptures was made into Greek. In later accounts the credit was given to none other than Ptolemy whose desire to know the teachings of the Jews caused him to have 70 scribes versed in Hebrew and

Greek brought from Jerusalem. This translation, the Septuagint, was to become the common religious and literary possession of all Greek-speaking Jews, and was to be the scripture out of which Christianity, under Paul and others in the Apostolic tradition, drew their knowledge. But there may also be another reason for the translation of the Scriptures into Greek: Jews in this Diaspora had lost their Hebrew and Aramaic as well and had no access to them. Greek had already become the lingua franca of the commercial classes and intelligentsia. If the Rabbis were correct in their understanding of the relationship between language and *souls*, then these Greek- speaking Jews were beginning to see a world that was quite different from that hedged in by the mountains of Judaea and the Mosaic Law.

Until 176 BCE, Jerusalem and Judaea remained on the periphery of urbanism. The High Priest, the Temple, its sacrifices and the priests who carried them out, were maintained and annual taxes submitted to the Kings of Antioch, for Coele-Syria lay within the Antiochean Seleucid Kingdom. In 176 BCE, Antiochus Epiphanes (IV) became king and almost immediately inaugurated a policy that was aimed at the forced Hellenization of his kingdom. Much of this concern was prompted by memory of his father's defeat by Rome and his attribution of this defeat to the disunified character of his lands. Unlike Egypt of the Ptolemys, Antiochean Syria had no tradition of god-kings, nor was its geography as favourable to unity. It was Antiochus who gave himself the name Theos Epiphanes: God made manifest. His primary aim was made apparent early in his reign: Judaea was to be made the base for any proposed attack on Ptolemaic Egypt, and was to be Hellenized at all costs. History has been unkind to Antiochus in many ways, not taking into account the fact that there were many Jews who saw things as he did. In Judaea, and more specifically in Jerusalem, many of the priests and members of both the old aristocracy and the new mercantile class chafed under restrictions that the Law of Moses imposed. The Jews were divided in their views of both the Greeks and their influence: some supported the incumbent High Priest Onias III and were traditionalists and faithful to the Mosaic Law, whilst others, led by a descendant of the High Priest Simon I, were for updating Jerusalem in accordance with the times. The latter spoke Greek, many had Greek names, and they followed Greek athletic games. This faction caused Onias to flee to Egypt in 176 and Antiochus appointed a new High Priest in the person of Joshua-Jason, a brother of Onias but a Hellenist. A gymnasium was constructed in Jerusalem and the Greek custom of performing naked in the games was introduced. Priests were found active in these games and even went so far as to have their circumcisions disguised. These feeble and uncomfortable endeavours, however, were not enough for Antiochus, and after dismissing Jason he appointed the latter's cousin, Menelaus-Onias, as the High Priest. As Menelaus-Onias's name indicates, he was a firm Hellenist.

In 169 BCE, Antiochus set out against Egypt and there followed a series of wars that almost led to his unifying Syria and Egypt united under his rule, but for the appearance of a Roman embassy led by Popilius Laenas. The Romans, fearing such a union, insisted that Antiochus retreat and in the course of this retreat he received news of a revolt in Judaea. The success of such a revolt would have destroyed the very buffer that he had been seeking in the area. After seizing Jerusalem and slaughtering the insurgents by the thousands, he proceeded to issue decrees in which the worship of the Judaean God was outlawed. Circumcision was forbidden and in 168 BCE, the Temple was turned over to the worship of the Greek Gods and swine were sacrificed on its altar. Their blood was then spattered on the exposed scrolls of the Law of Moses. It was in response to these horrors (to the traditionalist Jews), that in 166, a new revolt was led by Judah Maccabaeus. Aided to a degree by the sudden death of Antiochus, it was successful and in the following year Jerusalem was seized and the Temple re-dedicated to the worship of the Judaean God, an event that is commemorated to this day by Jews as the Feast of Hannuka.

It is in this conflict between Jew and Greek, that we can clearly see the problem that was going to face Jews in the Greco-Roman world. It is in this conflict that we can discern the irreconcilable differences that were to separate Jew and Gentile in Antiquity. The two were almost incapable of reaching accord—at least in Judaea. The impact of these events had a far reaching and profound impact on Jewish history, for out of it arose the Pharisees as a rabbinic party of separatists who saw even the Maccabees as having been ultimately seduced by Greek culture. If Josephus is correct, it was also not long after that the Essenes withdrew from the religious life of the people and formed closed communities of their own. This period, however, also saw a steady stream of emigration from Judea to the cities of the Greek Diaspora. If Hellenism was infiltrating into Judaea, a reciprocal process was taking place in which Jews now began to settle in great numbers in the cities of the Greek Diaspora. Alexandria, Antioch, Damascus and the cities of the hinterland became what well may have been havens for Hellenized Jews who found the rigours of Judaean religious life too much for their liking. It is also during the years following 150 BCE, that Jews began to settle as communities along the Western coast of Asia Minor, the Aegean, and in Greece. In the 1st century BCE, Strabo could mention as a matter of fact— rather than a question of surprise—that there was no city in the known world that did not have its Jews. The Greek Diaspora became the framework into which the Jewish Diaspora assumed its own form, a process that was going on as Rome systematically conquered the lands of the Near East, a process that saw the fall of Antiochean Syria, then Coele-Syria, and finally the absorption of Egypt into the Roman Empire in 30 BCE. By that time Alexandria, the Delta and Nile Valley, were to have up to a million Jews. It is estimated that by the 3rd century CE, that Jews numbered up to 10% of the total population of the Roman Empire.

The Jewish communities that were founded and developed during these centuries resembled each other closely and had similar institutions that united them. The synagogue was not only a place of worship but also functioned as a center in which the officers of the community could hold council, manage the legal affairs of the community and maintain various social services such as caring for widows and orphans, the maintaining a burial society, and providing facilities for ritually clean food. The language that united these communities was international Greek, the *koine*, and it is apparent that few Jews in the Diaspora knew Hebrew to any degree of proficiency. By the 1st century CE, the Alexandrine Jewish philosopher Philo could reveal with no embarrasment the fact that he knew no Hebrew and that his model in philosophic matters was Plato. It was Philo who worked out the Greek philosophical vocabulary that enabled Judaism to appear less strange and foreign than it did as revealed in the Septuagint. To the Gentile Greek, or Roman for that matter, the Septuagint was somewhat of a horror insofar as many intellectual Greeks found its anthropomorphism gross and its language crude. To make things worse it fit into no known category of literature: it was neither epic, drama, poetry, nor even history as the Greek understood the discipline. Philo's later Platonization of Jewish thought made it accessible to the Gentile world and no doubt assisted greatly in making Judaism attractive to many—which it was. Jews during this time were great proselytizers as Jesus himself remarks in reference to the zeal of the Pharisees who went to the ends of the earth to win a single Gentile convert while ignoring the religious wilderness that was Galilee. Already in many Jewish communities an interesting process was taking place in which Jews were being drawn more and more into intimate involvement with Gentiles and reciprocally Gentiles were being drawn closer and closer to Judaism:

attracted by its simplicity, its structured family life, though still repelled to a degree by circumcision and the food laws. Nonetheless, the Pharisees had themselves learned a great deal. Unlike the Sadduchees, they saw the God of Israel as Universal, and the Law, in its essential form—as summed up by the great Hillel—'Love the Lord thy God with all thy heart and all thy soul, and thy neighbor as thyself,'as applicable to all mankind. Still, to become a Jew meant a complete transformation of one's life, and there were many who could neither handle this nor condone it.

Paul of Tarsus was a Jew of this world, as was Stephen, whose very name indicates that he was probably of a Hellenizing background in Antioch. Paul's understanding of the teachings of Jesus of Nazareth, whom he never met, was focused, as one might expect, not within the narrow horizon of Jerusalem and Judaea, but within the vast world of the Roman Empire, which in turn was modeled on that of Alexander. Born in Tarsus as a Diaspora Jew, Paul had learnt his Greek as a young man and must have known Greeks and Romans intimately, even though he appears to have come from a religious family. Paul, in making explicit what he understood to be implicit in the teachings of the Nazarene, provided the basis for that form of Judaism accessible to the Gentile that we know of as Christianity. As a Jewish sect, Christianity had undergone a crisis not long after the death of Jesus in which inhibiting laws and restrictions were considered to be no longer applicable. Jew and Gentile alike were equal as children of God. It is significant that Paul's main journeys took him into the very heart of the Hellenistic world: to the cities of Ionian Asia Minor, Ephesus, Sardes, and on into Macedonia, Thessaloniki, Verroia, Athens and Corinth. It was in the Diaspora synagogues that he first preached; and it was in Greek that he formulated his ideas and later wrote his epistles.

In 71 CE, not long after the death of Paul of Tarsus in Rome, Jerusalem was razed to the ground by

17

the Romans and the Temple was destroyed. The Pharisee leader, R. Iohanan Ben Zakkai, who was smuggled out of the city just prior to its fall by means of a ruse, made his way to Jabne and there, with Roman support, set up the first center for restructuring Jewish life in a world with neither Jerusalem nor Temple. As time went on, this academy became the main point of contact between Roman officialdom and the Jews. It was here that the Oral law of the Jews, which according to tradition had been passed on from God to Moses and hence through a series of transmissions down to the Great Assembly, was finally put into writing. Eventually two works resulted from this process of collecting and codifying the traditions, customs, laws and attitudes that were what remained of the Jewish experience in time. The Palestinian Talmud is the oldest and shortest. Later, in Babylon—in another Diaspora quite different from that in the Greco-Roman world—the Babylonian Talmud emerged and became definitively authoritative for most Jews.

What is of interest during this period is that both Christianity and Judaism were making the necessary adjustments and self-definitions so as to create a mode of existence that enabled both to survive the disaster of the Fall of Jerusalem in 71 CE. For Christians this involved the search for authority, and an organization that expressed its view of itself as the New Israel. In the process, the Great Church developed an episcopal organization, the authority for whose teaching rested on a canon of Scripture that it shared with Jews: the Old Testament. To this were appended the four Gospel accounts, the Acts and the Letters of the Apostles. The message of the Church was rooted in Judaism but also, in a very dramatic and meaningful manner, went beyond it. Whereas Judaism had seen its history as a series of unique encounters between the Jews and God, Christianity saw these encounters as a preparation leading to the axial moment in the history of the entire universe that was redeemed from destruction and death by the sacrifice of the Son of God. The

18

Universe, since the sin of Adam had been unanchored in a sense and cast adrift from God. In His compassion God began to lay plans to redeem the Universe, singling out Noah, then Abraham, and, finally, the Children of Abraham as a special people to Him insofar as they maintained the Covenant that He made with them. In the fullness of time Jesus of Nazareth was born, the Incarnate Son or Logos of God, and in his sacrificial death the Universe was redeemed and the Law, or Covenant, fulfilled. As Messiah he had withdrawn from the world, and at an unknown time in the future, would return as the fully revealed Messiah to inaugurate the Millenium of Peace and Justice.

Christians, once baptized, were members of this New Israel--there was no difference within it between Jew and Gentile. What is especially striking about the Christian understanding of the life and death of Jesus is its use of Greek philosophical ideas, pagan mythological language and images as well as Roman legalisms. It was the Logos of God that had been made incarnate in the Law of Israel delivered to Moses on Mt. Sinai. It was this same Logos that had become incarnate in Jesus. Christianity was reworked within the language, images and concepts of the Greco-Roman world. By the reign of Constantine the Great (305-336)CE. the process was more or less capped. The Church was freed from constraints, the Emperor himself became Christian and hence the vicar, or incumbent, for the absent Messiah. In 331 Constantinople was founded as a Second Rome. It was destined as well to become in the religious imagery of the Christians, a Second Jerusalem for the New Israel. Later, with the building of Hagia Sophia in 536, Justinian himself summed up its significance as a temple unique in the Christian world by holding up his arms in the great church and crying *Solomon, I have outdone thee.* Here indeed was for Christians the restored Temple waiting for its future Messianic role. Constantinople was looked upon as being the shadow cast by the Heavenly Jerusalem, its emperor the vicar of the Messiah, Hagia Sophia the Temple and audience hall of almighty God in which He and His vicar met in great liturgical acts.

Parallel to Christian development, Jews were undergoing their own process of adjustment though it was in many ways much more difficult. The tragedy of 71 CE. contained for Jews no spark of hope as it did for Christians (either Jewish or Gentile). The latter saw it as a sign of the times, an indication that the time was approaching for the Messianic return (Parousia). For Jews it was a great punishment. Israel had failed again in its mission among the nations. It was even accounted that at the very moment when the Temple shuddered and then collapsed in the flames that the Levites mounted its pinnacles and threw the keys that had been entrusted to them into the sky crying that they had been unworthy of their office as its wardens.

Guilt and certainly inner contradictions placed a burden on Jews that could have destroyed them as a people had there not been precedents for survival in the flexible backbone of rabbinical Pharisaic teaching. Already at the time of Jesus, the Pharisees had seen a universal role for Judaism. Their teachings were openly aimed at making proselytes. They were teachers and their home was in the synagogues, in the academies. Rigid in their adherence to the ritual and Laws of the Covenant they saw the root of Jewish religious experience in being like God, in being righteous and just. It was this moral basis of Judaism that the Pharisees developed and which they taught in Hellenistic Diaspora. It was inevitable that they would come into conflict with their sister faith, Christianity. Ironically both shared the Septuagint and their polemics turned on variant readings of terms and the significance of prophetic writings. In response to this a new translation into Greek was made by the Jewish convert Aquila. Judaism also had the problem of finding authority to support the role of rabbis and the validity of their teachings. Whereas both the Temple and the priesthood were rooted in the Law of Moses as revealed om Mt. Sinai, the existence of both the Pharisaical rabbinate as well as the synagogue was not. Recourse was made to the Oral Law that had been developing for some centuries as a means of adapting the Written

20

Law (Torah, i.e. the Five Books of Moses) to new contingencies. In order to guarantee that they would not be accused of creating a second written Law, the Rabbis had, through repetition and memorization, created an enormous corpus of legal decisions, traditions and precedents that indicated the manner in which the Torah had been applied in temporal circumstances. This was called the Mishna. By the beginning of the 3rd century this began to be written down and under R. Juda Nasi it was *closed*. In two great centres of exiled Jewish life, Palestine and Babylon (which lay in Persian territory), the Mishna was studied and further commented on. This is not the place to enter into its history other than to say that by the middle of the 5th century this process also came to an end and there stood two interpretations and applications of the Mishna—that of the Palestinian academies sometimes called the Jerusalem Talmud and that of the Jews of Persia called the Babylonia Talmud. The Palestinian Talmud was authoritative in most Roman territories including Southern Italy until as late as the 12th century. In Greece some of its influence was felt as late as that 20th cent.

As the form of Christianity began to become more and more influenced by the Greco-Roman world through its converts and culture, Judaism tended to draw more and more into itself. The great disaster of the Bar Kochba revolt in the 2nd century CE. saw an end to the Jewish homeland and was, for Christians, a further sign of God's disfavor with the Old Israel. For nearly two thousand years Jews were to live their lives in accordance with the Laws and traditions as understood and applied, for the most part, by rabbinical authorities. We have only elusive evidence of what disappeared in terms of Jewish culture during these disastrous years. Jewish art as evidenced in the rich frescoes discovered in our century at Dura Europos ceased to play a part in synagogue decoration. Borrowings by Christian artists from illustrated Jewish texts of the Bible or the Jewish catacombs in Rome, not to mention synagogue floor mosaics found in Eretz and

21

in many parts of the Roman world are but remnants of a tradition in the arts that was decisively terminated. As Christian art grew and developed, Jewish art reciprocally, and no doubt by way of reaction, ceased to exist.

In general, the Jews of the Roman Empire began to fare badly after the conversion of Constantine the Great to Christianity. They were, however, within the protection and confines of Roman Law. Despite what was considered their error in not having accepted Jesus as the Messiah, they were the People of God. In fulfilling His Law, they maintained their part of the Covenant. There was Old Israel and New Israel and in some strange sense the Jews were thus considered to be within the Church. (This was especially true in the West where this view was refined by St. Augustine in the early 5th century).

Between the latter part of the 4th and the middle part of the 8th centuries, covering a period of some three hundred years, the structure and character of the Greco-Roman World of Late Antiquity changed. First there were the Germanic Invasions beginning in 368 which saw, by the middle of the 5th century, the complete breakup of Roman authority in the West, save for southern Italy. Not long after that the Islamic Invasions began, and between 634 and 750 CE, all of the Near Eastern and North African provinces of the Empire fell to Islam. What remained of the Roman Empire was centered in the southern Balkans, and sections of Anatolia. This now can be accurately called the Byzantine Empire, as its capital was at Byzantium or Constantinople. The only living legitimate tradition that could trace its authority and culture directly back to the Antiquity was this remnant of the once mighty Rome. Its Jews, speaking Greek, which was by now the official language of the Empire, were Roman Jews or Romaniots. Under the Germanic states of the West Greek ceased to be the international language of the cultured classes. Latin took its place and Germanic and Romance *vulgar* languages developed. In the East, and North Africa, Greek was replaced by Arabic which became itself a new international language.

By this time most of the Jewish communities in Greece were very ancient. Many of them, such as those of Crete, Halkis, Thessaloniki and elsewhere, could even defend themselves against Christian attacks that they were deocides by pointing out that their ancestors had settled where they were long before the death of Jesus in Jerusalem: they were almost, in this sense, autochthonous.

Our knowledge of Romaniot Jewish life during these years is almost non- existent and reflects a lacuna in Byzantine history that was undoubtedly caused by the Slavic invasions into the Balkans, the conquest of Crete by the Arabs and the arrival of the Bulgarians into Byzantine lands on either side of the Danube River. This absence of information is so complete that it has led many scholars to accept the distinct possibility that for over a century most of what we call Greece today had been lost to these invaders. But we do have hints of Jewish communities that apparently weathered the stormy centuries. Some at Krissa (near Delphi) apparently were agrarian. This was the case also with the Jews of certain parts of Crete where the Jewish communities were divided: some being urban and others being agrarian. It is most likely that there were few differences between the lives of the Christian and Jewish communities. Greek was certainly the common language and had become for the Jews so much a part of their lives that parts of the Romaniot liturgy were read in Greek. The five megilloth of Esther, Ruth, Lamentations, etc. were usually recited in Greek though (from religious nostalgia) using the Hebrew alphabet. The influence of the Palestinian Talmud and peculiarities imposed by life in the Empire led to the development of what became known as the Minhag Romania (Greek Rite). Sadly, this passed out of existence in the period following the arrival of the Sephardic Jews, and today survives only in the memories of very old people who either remember, or still have written down in copy books some of the special prayers and piyyutim that were peculiar to it. It is of interest as well that many of these texts are still to be found written in Greek but using the Hebrew alphabet, right up to our own century.

During the 10th and early 11th centuries the Empire saw its fortunes change with an accession of a number of energetic Emperors. After the breakup of the Bulgarian Kingdom, their efforts were spent largely on re- Hellenizing Greece. What this involved was the absorption of the various tribal peoples, Slavs, Bulgarians and others, who had settled in the Balkans. These were now subject to a vigorous programme of *Byzantinization*: through conversion to Orthodoxy, the adoption of Greek and the acceptance of the Emperor. It was inevitable that some of this process affected the Jews and during this time we have mention of a number of weak attempts to convert the Jews forcibly to Christianity through Imperial Edicts.

These efforts may well have been successful in certain areas. There are still groups of Greek Christians—Maniotes and Tsakones being two, who claim Jewish ancestry. (The Vlachs when still semi- nomadic maintained a similar view of themselves, though that might have arisen out of an early near conversion to Judaism. Nonetheless, it is interesting and significant that a number of foreign visitors to Greece in the late 17th century remarked that the Vlachs, when raiding would both plunder and murder, unless the victim happened to be a Jew, in which case they would only steal from him).

By the 11th century the fortunes of the Empire had recovered and this is reflected in the growth of certain urban areas such as Thessaloniki and in a more stable Jewish economic identification. In Thebes the Jews were mainly involved in the production and dying of silk, which had become a stable source of Imperial revenues. The community was quite large and important enough to cause debate and comment amongst

24

rabbinical visitors from the West over the question of *sha'tnaz* (the law prohibiting the mixture of linen and wool in a woven textile). The Theban Jews applied this law by analogy to the use of hemp in weaving either wool or silk, a subtlety in interpretation that was unknown among the Jews of the West.

Marriage customs among Romaniot Jews also apparently caused some consternation among visiting Rabbis. It was customary to have the Seven Blessings read at a betrothal after which the couple were allowed to cohabit for a year. At the end of the year the *Ketubah* (marriage contract) was read at the proper wedding. The irregularity of this custom, which may have been influenced to some degree by Christian practice, also affected the dowry settlement should the actual marriage not take place. Other problems arose over the manner of building and using the *mikve* (ritual bath).

Consequent to a series of successful incursions into Abbasid-held eastern Anatolia, the Byzantines managed to recapture several cities such as Antioch and Aleppo. In reabsorbing these cities and the hinterland they also re-incorporated large Jewish Communities that had been, for some years, within Islam. It appears that many Jews, taking advantage of the atmosphere of tolerance and the general economic revival in Byzantium made their way to western Anatolia, Greece, Macedonia, and Thrace. Significant numbers of Karaites also emigrated and settled in Thessaloniki and Constantinople and stimulated debate and concern among rabbinical Jews. The Karaites were/are an alternative Jewish adaption to life in the Diaspora without Temple and without Homeland. They had no Oral Law, or Talmud, hence application of the Torah was limited to its literal interpretation. This is an attitude not unlike that of the Sadduchees from which they may, in fact, have descended.

During the preceding centuries Greek Jewry had suffered under invasions and periodic persecutions that had no doubt limited intellectual activities. Many of the new arrivals, on the other hand, had seen more stable conditions and their understanding of the Law, or Torah, was based on the more detailed and labyrinthine paths of the Babylonian Talmud; as opposed to that of Palestine, which was still appealed to by Greek Jews. Mention should also be made of the fact that Greek Jews in many cases approached the interpretation of the Law directly and not by recourse to Talmudic views. This perhaps also made them less inimical to Karaites who refused to consider either of the Talmuds. Certainly these new Jews must have caused tension in the pre- existing Jewish communities of Byzantine lands.

The Byzantine recovery was, however, short-lived. Incursions of Normans from Sicily into the Peloponessos affected Jewish life. From Thebes several thousand silk weavers and dyers were kidnapped by the Normans and carried off to Sicily in order to introduce silk production there. Internal crises in Islamic lands were complicated by the establishment of a Seljuq Turkish Sultanate at Baghdad and in 1077 CE, they routed a Byzantine army at Manzikert, thus opening the interior of Asia Minor and creating within a short period of time the Seljuq Sultanate of Rum. It was in response to this event that the Emperor Alexis appealed to the West, an appeal which was to result in the 1st Crusade. The initial religious enthusiasm of the Crusaders was but a thin veneer over deeper and more mundane incentives. Within a short period of time Jerusalem was taken by the 1st Crusade, and the horrors that accompanied its fall were to make the word Frank a term of abhorrence in the Near East even into modern times. In the course of the first three Crusades, the armies of the West only passed through Byzantine territory, but in the course of these passages both they and the Byzantines developed a mutual distrust that was further exacerbated by the fact that in the middle of the 11th century the Churches of Rome and Constantinople had fallen into schism.

We know too well how the Jews of Europe fared at this time. Those of Byzantium were, of course, protected by Roman Law and what debilities there were did not appreciably interfere with certain rights viz. even to the point of land ownership.

We have a good picture of Jewish life in Byzantium that was drawn for us by Benjamin of Tudela, a Gem merchant from Spain, who arrived in Western Greece via Otranto in 1167. It is from Benjamin that we get a view of the dispersion of the Jews in various towns of Greece as well as into the islands. He mentions the wealthy community of Thebes and its involvement in the silk trade and its population of Jews, which exceeded two thousand persons. After a stay in Constantinople, he made his way via the islands down the coast of Asia Minor and from there continued into the Near East in 1172. In his account it is interesting to find that he does not mention Jews in towns and cities where one might have expected him to, e.g. Athens, and Ioannina, though this may have been determined by the route that he took rather than an absence of Jews in these towns.

In 1204 the 4th Crusade, under the leadership of Venice, turned its attention and interests to Christian Constantinople and after the conquest of the City the Empire was divided between the various participants. Venice seized the lion's share by acquiring the central Aegean Islands, some of the key ports in Greece and the islands of Crete, and those of the Ionian Sea. Three Byzantine centers in exile—at Nicaea, in Epirus, and at Trebizond—maintained the continuity of Byzantine traditions but for the most part the Empire was now Frankish. The Jews were severely restricted, economic life began to wither and in Venetian held territories they suffered restrictions that they had not known before. That peculiar invention of the Serenissimo, the ghetto, was imposed on Jewish communities in Crete, Corfu, and elsewhere.

Despite these debilities many Jews undoubtedly

took advantage of Venetian contacts and markets to benefit economically. Kosher wines and cheeses from Crete were famous and exported to Jewish communities of Europe via Venice. We know as well that after the recapture of Constantinople by the Byzantines, many Cretan Jews preferred to claim Venetian identity and to live (if they could) within the Venetian Quarter of Galata. What also most likely benefited these 'Venetian' Jews was the creation of a Venetian maritime Empire that rested on the closely associated ports of Corinth, Modon, Candia, and Zakynthos.

In other Crusader-held sections of Greece, Jewish life was brought almost to a standstill. Unlike the Venetians, the other participants in the in-famous Fourth Crusade, invested poorly in their newly acquired territories. Cities became depopulated and economic life based on trade and international commerce was unproductive and was severely retarded by the introduction of an already antiquated feudalism that little suited either the history or the character of the lands they held. Essentially what was created was a form of primitive colonialism in which fiefs were exploited and accumulated wealth sent back to Europe to be used by encumbants who, after 'retirement', were replaced by younger relatives. It is very possible that many Jews retreated into the countryside so as to escape direct interaction with the Crusaders.

The Byzantine recovery began in 1261 when the Emperor Michael VIII Palaeologos seized Constantinople and was crowned in Hagia Sophia. The capture of the City by no means ended the Crusader or Venetian presence and their complete removal from Greece was never really achieved. In areas where they were forced to depart, the consequences of the occupation were horrendous and everywhere apparent. In Constantinople, most of the churches had been sacked and left in ruins, the lead roofs stripped, the mosaics pillaged for gold, the relics broken up and sold or removed to churches in Europe. The Hippodrome and great palace of the Daphne were in ruins, and the hundreds of bronze statues that had once graced the former had been melted down into ingots. Some, such as the great bronze horses now in St. Mark's in Venice, had found new homes.

Faced with an empty treasury and a depopulated capital Michael quickly set about revitalizing the urban economies of Constantinople, Thessaloniki and other peripheral cities. His initial attempts were successful and included efforts to attract Jews to resettle in the cities. It is due to these attractions that Romaniot Jewry in the Empire entered into its last phase of creativity. Evidence concerning scholarly and religious life of Jews during this period is rich by comparison with earlier periods. A number of rabbinical scholars, such as Shemarya Ha-Ikriti, and his student Judah ibn Moskoni, were typical of the times. Both were trained Talmudists and writers of homilies and commentaries on the Scriptures. They were both cognizant as well of other contemporary sciences. Shemarya was proficient in medicine as well as philosophy, and Moskoni travelled widely in search of manuscripts and was especially important for his work in editing the scattered work of Abraham ibn Ezra. It is to him that we owe the best extant copy of the *Sefer Josiphon*..

The relatively secure conditions prevailing within the Empire began to attract immigrant Jews from the West. The first Sephardic (Iberian) Jews began to arrive shortly after the anti-Jewish incidents in Spain that occurred in 1391, and more followed on their heels in 1415. These early Sephardic immigrants settled in Crete, Constantinople, and Adrianople where they were given assistance by the Romaniots. During this time as well, numbers of Ashkenazic (European) Jews sought refuge in Thessaloniki and Constantinople where they established synagogues and quarters of their own. Resident Romaniot Jews provided these newcomers with texts and translations, as well as financial aid in establishing themselves. Internally the Romaniots finally reached a modus vivendi with the large Karaite community that had for centuries been problematic to them, and a comfortable coexistence was established that appears to have been a source of contention with the newcomers from Europe and elsewhere for whom the Karaites were anathema.

If the fortunes of the Jews within the borders of the re-established Byzantine Empire were improving, conditions were not reciprocally propitious in the territories surrounding it. In the early 14th cent. the Ottoman Turks had established themselves in northwestern Anatolia taking advantage of the vacuum that ensued following the break-up of the Seljuq Turkish Sultanate of Rum, and the Mongolian Invasions. Not long after establishing their capital at Bursa they were enlisted by the Byzantines as mercenaries against pretenders in Thrace. In 1361, after seizing Adrianople, the Turks became centered in Europe. From there they now carried on wars with Serbia and Bulgaria, as well as with the Byzantines to the east. The new Ottoman capital was renamed Edirne and under Sultan Murad II it began to attract artisans, intellectuals, technicians, scholars and poets many of whom were Jews and Christians as well as Muslims. The original community of Romaniot Jews was now significantly augmented by Jewish immigrants from Spain and Hungary. It is worth noting that Edirne, despite being Turkish, attracted such scholars as Gemistos Plethon and other Hellenists taking part in the remarkable and short-lived Hellenist revival of the time.

By 1445 it was evident to all that Constantinople was destined to be absorbed into the Ottoman Empire. It had already been reduced to paying an annual tribute to the Turks so as to maintain what in fact was a fiction of autonomy. One tends automatically to think of the fall of Empires in terms of the norms of a tragic drama, attempting to find the fatal flaw in an otherwise impeccable character. To watch the demise of a great Empire, brought about by some fatal inner contradiction ironically provides us with an illusion of security: permitting us to deceive ourselves by thinking that our age might be saved by our mediocrity. The last years of Christian Constantinople were neither edifying nor great. On the eve of its fall, Constantinople and what remained of the Empire, was a city marked by strange omens of disaster that caused many of its inhabitants to flee. Its population was seriously divided between those including the Emperor who had accepted Union with the Church of Rome as a means of acquiring assistance from the West, and the monastic and lesser clergy, as well as the majority of the common folk, who not only refused to accept the Union, but had also for some years refused to pray in the great church of Hagia Sophia. The Church was so seriously divided that it had been impossible to find a person agreed upon by all to fill the vacant Patriarchal throne. Many urged the Emperor to capitulate to the Turks and to move to the Pelponessos where a stronghold of Byzantine authority held on at Mistra. Sultan Murad himself promised the independance of a Greek Kingdom there with the Palaeologues as rulers should they surrender the City. Many, like Notaras, an immediate relative of the Emperor, felt that the Turkish turban was preferable to the Papal Tiara. Constantinople was an island in a Turkish sea. Through conversion and subsequent Turkification of large portions of the population of Thrace and Bythinia the City had been completely disengaged from its territories and people.

From what little is known of Jewish fortunes at this time it appears that some but not all Jews had begun to leave Constantinople for cities such as Edirne, Mistra, and perhaps even Venetian-held Crete. This evacuation of the City was not limited to them; and many of the aristocracy and higher clergy made their way even to the West, especially to Italy.

In 1453, on the 29th of May, the young Mehemt II seized the City after a short seige and the last Emperor was killed in the course of the fighting. Early on the following morning, Hagia Sophia was formally converted into a mosque when Mehmet prayed on what had been its altar. It is impossible for us in the late 20th century to grasp even faintly the impact of Mehmet's conquest of the great City. Constantinople was heir to ancient Rome, and to the sophisticated urban civilization of Greece. It was also New Rome, and at the a reflection of the Heavenly Jerusalem that Christians, as the New Israel, saw themselves citizens of. For many, the fall of Constantinople was a sign of the beginning of the end of the world. Reading into scripture or even into ancient prophecies and omens, the Greek-speaking Romaniot Jews could find a strange justice. Constantinople, the New Rome, the lineal heir to the Empire that had seen the destruction of Jerusalem and its Temple in 71 CE, had itself now fallen. If Christians began to read the signs of the times as prophetic of the Second Coming of the Messiah, Jews were equally prone to seeking such signs as could be found in scripture alluding to the Messianic Coming that had been awaited for hundreds of years. There was also, however, an atmosphere of bewilderment and despair. In the summer of 1453, a Jew of Candia, in Crete, R. Michael B. Shabbetai Kohen Balbo, wrote a Hebrew lament over the fall of the City in which he associated the fate of the Jews with that of the Greeks: 'For my people is taken captive in a great captivity along with my enemy...From heaven to earth has fallen the morning star to utter destruction. (Is. 52:2 & Ps. 65:8, Is. 14:12).

Mehmet was an extraordinary and complicated man, neither ignorant of history nor of the role that he had assumed as the Conqueror of the City. Islamic tradition had its own prophecies concerning its fall in the Quran, and there had been many attempts to seize it for almost a thousand years. Mehmet with some justification, saw himself as an intrument of destiny and accordingly he took his role seriously. On the firm foundations that he laid, Constantinople was in less than a century to become the richest city in the world and the capital of an Empire that stretched from the gates of Vienna to Iran and across North Africa into the Arabian Peninsula.

One of his first acts was to stabilize conditions as much as possible. The most immediate problem was the question of the various minorities or *dimmis* (non-Muslims) who had been absorbed into the Ottoman state. *Sharia*(Islamic Law) based as it was on the Qur'an could not be applied to unbelievers. Following precedents established as early as the 7th century, these *dimmis* had the right to religious freedom as well as a modicum of legal independence. Their liability was the payment of a heavy tax that could and did in times of stress provide an incentive for conversion to Islam.

Under Mehmet, the Christian community was immediately organized under a newly appointed. Patriarch in the person of George Gennadios, who as a monk had also been the head of the anti-Imperial and Union party in Constantinople. He was now made the chief representative of the Christian *millet*. Ironically, the tragedy of the fall of Constantinople became the beginning of one of the richest periods in the history of the Orthodox Church. The authority of the Patriarchs of Constantinople once again extended over Christians who had lived within the confines of the Islamic world since the 7th century.

For the Jews, a similar head was appointed in Moses Kapsalis, a Cretan Rabbi, who had been resident in the City for several years, and who had been there when it fell. While organizing the *millets*, Mehmet also conscripted Christian and Jewish families from Asia Minor and Thrace to settle in various cities. Thessaloniki was given its quota of Jews and many of the older communities elsewhere began to flourish and grow in the Pax Ottomanica. Until the very end of Byzantium, its Jews had lived in a Christian milieu and the focus of attention, despite various religious and military problems, had been directed to the Christian West. As a consequence of these recent and dramatic changes, the Greek-speaking Jews found themselves in an Empire that very quickly expanded further into the East and North Africa, and in doing so absorbed

Jewish communities that had lived for centuries within the relatively tolerant atmosphere of Islam. Romaniot Jewry was now drawn into the world of Islamic Judaism. New economic ties were established with Alexandria, Djerba, Beirut, and other active cities in the Near East. Access to Eretz and the Holy City was comparatively easy.

Perhaps the most important consequence of these great changes was the stability it gave to Jewish lives and fortunes. The reconstruction of economic life under Mehmet created at the same time the bases of havens into which vast numbers of Sephardic Jews, fleeing Spain,toward the end of the l5th century were to find stable communities in which to begin establishing themselves.

The expulsion of the Jews from Spain in 1492 was the result of two factors: a significant change in the attitude of the Church towards Jews and an incipient form of nationalism that at this stage of its development can best be called *nativism*.

The position of the Western Catholic Church towards the Jews was significantly different from that of the Eastern Church of Byzantium. This distinction is of prime importance in understanding the position of Jews in the East and West of Christendom. There is no doubt that Byzantine Romaniot Jews suffered at times. Attempts at forced conversions were rare and in some instances—as in the period during the 9th and 10th centuries—they were the outcome of Imperial policy which could, and often did, run counter to the dogmas and attitudes of the Church itself. During the 12th century, Benjamin of Tudela notes the large number of Jews who lived in provincial towns of Greece and their comparative freedom of action and ownership of land and property. He was, however, shocked at the treatment of Jews in Constantinople, noting that on occasion they were publically beaten, that they were isolated in one quarter called Pera, and the odium attached to their main form of economic activity which

34

was tanning. One must keep in mind that Benjamin was from Tudela in Spain and had not experienced such debilities, and was hence justifiably disturbed by them. It must also be born in mind that from his general description of life in Byzantine territories, most of the Jews lived not in the cities such as Constantinople and Thessaloniki, but in smaller towns where they were obviously better off through either indifferent or better relations with their neighbors. Despite the fact that they were classed as heretics, the Jews of Byzantium were within the sphere of protection of Roman Law in its many re-codifications. It was not until the Crusades introduced a different attitude towards Jews that this atmosphere changed.

In Europe, i.e. the Western Germanic Nations, until the late 11th century, Jews for the most part enjoyed a kind of protection by the Church. The position of the Jews within Christendom had been theologically worked out by Augustine of Hippo in the 5th century, who saw the Jews as the 'Old Israel' still bearing witness to the Covenant made at Sinai, alongside the 'New Israel' which was the Church. The fact that the Jews had not accepted Jesus as the Messiah and had been responsible for his death, did nothing to change the fact that the original Covenant had been made between them and God on Sinai, and was expressed by fulfilling its laws and injunctions. Christians may not have liked the Jews, but little could be done as long as they maintained, even in ignorance, the Law that their ancestors had agreed to in good faith. In some peculiar manner the Jews were considered to be within the Church, whether they liked this locus or not.

A decided change in this attitude began to take place in the 11th century, not long after the First Crusade. In the writings of Anselm of Canterbury (+1109), and of Peter the Venerable (+1156), the approach to Christian Jewish polemics switched from the use of the common Scriptures to attacks on a source to which Jews often had recourse while arguing with

35

Christians: the Talmud. Until the 11th century the Talmud was unknown to Christians other than by name. Ignorance of the language in which it was written, plus complete ignorance as to what role it played (or 'he' played, as many Christians had the impression that Talmud was a man) made Jewish appeals to this written oral law a mystery until it was found that Jews, for the most part, understood and fulfilled the Law of Moses (the Written Law of God) through the Oral Law that had accrued in the course of centuries in the Talmud. The Talmud was admittedly man made and no Jew would have even suggested that it was revealed. If this were the case, and if, as was in fact the case, Jews followed peculiar interpretations of obscure passages in scripture that were based on Rabbinic decisions found in the Talmud, then Jews were not living according to the Law of God. They were, ipso facto heretics and the punishment for the heretic was quite different that that in Byzantium. In the former they were burnt, in the latter banishment in extreme cases was the worst that could happen. The public condemnation of the Talmud, and its burning in 1239 under the order of Pope Gregory IX, saw the Jews excluded from normal society and protection in the West. It is ironically tragic that this official act of the Church, which was to have far reaching repercussions on the Jews of Europe was prompted by the Jewish community of Montpelier, which, in 1232 had appealed to the ecclesiastical authorities to assist them in the condemnation of the works of the Aristotelian Moses ibn Maimon (Maimonides). Shortly after the burning of the *Mishneh Torah* and the *Guide for the Perplexed* Rabbi Joseph ben Todros ha-Levi Abulafia of Toleda was to comment '...it is certainly not right when they (the Jews) carry their controversy for judgement to our lord the bishop... This is what led to the burning of this book(s) by the clergy...'

At almost the same time, the Roman Church's stand as the legitimate heir to Roman universalism, as formulated under the great reforming Popes of the 11th century, was being challenged by strong national and

regional monarchies. Accompanying these develop-
ments were ideas and aspirations that were nativistic.
Nativism is a primitive form of nationalism and is
more in the nature of an attitude of mind than a theory
of state. From its point of view, anyone who has
interests, allegiances and concerns that are outside
those of the majority of a particular society is considered not only a bad citizen but also a threat. With the
breakup of the universal authority of the Roman
Church in the West, the Jew found himself exposed as
a heretic, but also, due to his position as a member of a
distinctly different social and religious affiliation, an
enemy of the community.

Until the 13th century Spain had a history that
was more closely linked to Africa than to Europe. Its
large Jewish community had flourished under the
Umayyad Caliphate of Cordoba and later, under
minor Muslim princes. It was little prepared for the
intrusion of nativistic ideas.

We do not know when the first Jews arrived in the
Iberian peninsula, but they were certainly there in the
1st century. We can assume that they were Greek
speaking and Roman oriented. With the conversion of
the Empire to Christanity, the Jewries of Spain fell
under restrictive, though not anti- semitic, laws established by Constantine the Great. Occasional Christian
synods in Spain made life difficult for the Jews but
hardly oppressive. In the early 5th century Spain was
conquered, first by the Vandals, and shortly after by
the Visigoths, who drove the former into North Africa.
The Jews did not fare well under the Visigoths which
was probably due to the fact that the Visigoths were
themselves despised by the Romans whom they had
conquered, and though Christian had adopted its
Arian form which was considered heretical. The Jew
apparently got the worst part of response from this
defective Visigothic self-image. In the 7th century
almost all of Spain was conquered by the Muslims and
the Jews found themselves in the much more tolerant
atmosphere of Dar ul-Islam (The Abode of Islam).

They became involved in all of the professions, were technicians, doctors and farmers as well as tradesmen. Some became great rabbis and philosophers. There is much justification for speaking of the glory of Spanish Jewry in the middle ages.

All of this began to change when Christian princes in the north of Spain saw and took the advantage of serious dynastic squabbles among the Muslim states in the south and began the *reconquista.*.

Subsequent to the successful wars of the Christian princes, Iberian Jews and Muslims either fled south or, more usually, remained where they were. In so doing they found themselves in a much less tolerant atmosphere, one that was formed by attitudes toward non-Christians resembling those of the Crusaders. In the beginning, the main brunt of the force of the Reconquista was directed toward warring Muslim states, but as these fell one by one the Jews (and Muslims) within their midst began to suffer restrictions.

In 1391 these restrictions were followed by a breakout of open persecution that saw the deaths of thousands and the forced or willing conversions of others to Christianity. They were known as *conversos*, or more derogatively Marranos. Many appear to have become sincere Christians, as is the case of the families of the great Christian mystics, St. Therese of Avila and St.John of the Cross. Others chose conversion as a means of saving their fortunes or in order to take advantage of the financial and social opportunities offered by being Christians. Many adhered only superficially to Christianity and secretly followed Jewish laws and ritual where and if they could. Those who were sincere rose high in Spanish life and society, as did those whose sincerity appears to have been doubtful. Distinctly problematic were the crypto-Jews who could, with theological justification, be defined as proper heretics or apostates. Increasingly the Jews began to suffer under growing nativism that saw them as members of a suspect socio-religious group or as heterodox Christians.

In 1483, the Dominican Thomas Torquemada, ironically a member of a converso family, was appointed Grand Inquisitor for Spain. His special role was to weed out and destroy heretical elements in the Spanish Church, and the trials and condemnations were aimed specifically at the Marranos. Talmudic Jews could not be dealt with by the Inquisition as they were outside the religious jurisdiction of Canon Law. European kings had set precedents for dealing with this problem—-expulsions. The wandering and home-less Jew had become a well-enough-known figure.

In 1492 the last Muslim stronghold at Granada was captured and in the spring of that year Ferdinand and Isabella issued the Edict of Expulsion, whereby all Muslims and Jews were given three months to sell their property and leave Spain. On July 31, 1492 the last ship bearing what was left of some two hundred thousand Jews left Spain. The Jews who remained were Marannos and were to be harassed by the Inquisition until as late as the 18th and early 19th century. Jews fleeing Spain made their way into North Africa, the Papal States and Eretz. A great number of them made appeals to the Ottoman Sultan, Beyazid II, the son of Mehmet II. Almost immediately the request for asylum was granted and he is credited with having said: How foolish of the monarchs of Spain to impover-ish their empire while enriching my own.

We have no idea as to the exact numbers of Jews who arrived from Spain and later, from Portugal into Ottoman lands. In some cities the number must have been proportionately very great. Thessaloniki, Bel-grade, Edirne, Constantinople, Bursa, and Izmir saw a great influx. For anyone who had lived during the past fifty or sisty years or so, these must have been fascinat-ing times. A Romaniot Jew living in Constantinople, or any other city that fell to the Turks after 1450, would have been witness to the fall of the City, the incursion, of the Turks and then its Turkification. In these new conditions he would have seen Jewish fortunes take a positive turn. Jews were being officially assisted in settling in cities. They were free to participate in trade, and in religious matters they were left alone. Now, fifty years later, the Empire had become a haven for Jews—but Jews of quite a strange type. Many of the new arrivals were from the south of Spain, and thus part of what could be called Moghrebi, or North African Jewry. Others were from the north or central Spain and had already benefited or been influenced by the rich sophisticated life of the Rennaissance. Still others were Marranos who may have left due to some sudden burst of Jewishness, of enthusiasm, or of fear at being discovered. These especially must have had a difficult time, as their knowledge of the religion and customs of their ancestors was based on surviving memories or customs rather than the hard rigors of Jewish Law.

The new arrivals were given every assistance by the urban Romaniots, but it was not long before differences in language, social customs and the fact that Romaniot Jews were considered to be culturally backward, resulted in friction. In Thessaloniki the new arrivals very quickly outnumbered the Romaniots who were now forced to learn Spanish as well as adapt themselves to new customs. That this process affected their sense of survival is shown by the fact that the Romaniot Siddur was formalized at this time, no doubt in order to keep it from being lost. A new printing of the Bible in Greek and Ladino was also brought out in Constantinople. There is no doubt that from this date onward the Romaniot Jews enter into a cultural and spiritual decline from which they never recovered. Spanish, or Sephardic Jewry was to almost completely eradicate some Romaniot communities or to fan differences that were to keep the two communites quite distinct. The term Grego in Spanish, could be used to designate either a Greek or, more derogatively, a Romaniot Jew.

Some of this feeling of superiority may well have been a consequence of the quite different manner in which these two communities were considered in Ottoman society. The Romaniot Jew, from the point of view of an Ottoman, had been conquered and his very Greekness may well have been a source of repulsion. On the other hand, the Spanish Jews had not been conquered. Refugees they may have been, but they had arrived as free persons and accepted asylum with certain privileges that Romaniot Jews did not enjoy. It should also be kept in mind that many Spanish Jews, born and brought up in the exciting Renaissance atmosphere of the 15th century, knew Latin, Italian, French, and Spanish. Many certainly were what we would call assimilated, and still others were only dimly aware of what being Jewish involved. Many were technicians, craftsmen, gunsmiths, gold workers, map makers and creators of fine navigational instruments. Others were doctors and bankers or printers. The Sepharadim brought with them a higher level of culture and general achievement than that of the Romaniot Jews. This certainly enhanced their self image as well as the attitude that the Ottomans had towards them.

The movement of Marrano Jews into the Empire continued well into the 16th century. While not typical, as she was enormously wealthy, the passage of Dona Gracia Mendes provides some picture of what this entailed. Dona Gracia was born in Lisbon in 1510 into a Marrano family and received the name Beatrice de Luna. While quite young she was married to a wealthy banker and gem merchant by the name of Francisco Mendes, also a Marrano, and on his death in 1537, she inherited his vast and well- invested fortune. Mendes had several commercial and banking contacts in London and Antwerp, and his widow, having determined to leave Portugal and return to Judaism, shrewdly began to transfer her fortune out of Portugal. In a few years she made her way to Antwerp, via London, accompanied by her daughter, Reyna, and nephew, Joao Micas, as well as her household. After some time in Antwerp she apparently set plans in motion to move further east. Setting out for Venice in 1545, she eventually settled in Ferrara, and there proclaimed her Jewishness and took the name of Gracia Nasi. Her nephew following suit assumed the name of Jose Nasi, and a few years later he and Reyna (now known as Dona Gracia la Chica) were married.

During these years Dona Gracia provided vast sums of money to assist fleeing Jews from Spain and Portugal in finding haven either by moving into Papal protection in Italy, or further east. In 1553 the great Ferrara Bible was dedicated to her as well as the *Consolation for the Tribulations of Israel* by Samuel Usques. Roth, in his biography of Dona Gracia likens her influence and involvement in Jewish fortunes to the great Queen Esther. Probably in 1555 she herself crossed over into the Ottoman-held Balkans. After spending a short period of time in Thessaloniki, she made her way to Constantinople. The Sultan (Suleiman) gave her extraordinary privileges including a house, lands in Galata, and the right to wear European dress. Until her death in 1569, she was tireless in her work for the settlement of Jews and established schools and synagogues not only in Constantinople, but as far east as Eretz Israel where (in Tiberius) she possibly died and was buried.

The influence of Jews in the Ottoman Court was especially high at this time. The wife of Selim, son and heir of Suleiman, who was to become the second Sultan to bear that name, was a Jewess, Nur Banu. One of her closest confidantes was the famous Esther Kyra, who was so involved in the intrigues of the Harem that she was ultimately killed by the Yeniceris. Don Jose quickly rose in this milieu to become the closest companion to Selim. His influence on Selim may not have been entirely wholesome as the Sultan was given the nick- name of the Sot, and it is known that Don Jose procured wine for his table. He also enjoyed the guarded favour of the Grand Vizier, Sokullu Mehmet.

Leading the anti-Venetian party it was they who worked behind the scenes to extend Ottoman power by conquering Venetian holdings in the Aegean as well as conquering the island of Cyprus. For his efforts, and influence, Don Jose was rewarded by being made Duke of Naxos and there is an interesting possibility that he attempted to obtain the Island of Cyprus as a homeland for the Jews. Failing in this, he concentrated much of his energies in later life in making Tiberius a strongly Jewish town, and endowed, along with his mother-in-law cum aunt Dona Gracia, many foundations.

While it is true that the vast majority of Jews settled in Constantinople, it was the city of Salonika (Thessaloniki) that assumed almost a totally Jewish character. Undoubtedly, the response of the successors of Selim to what was truly a Jewish cabal in the Court, contributed to a contraction in Jewish efforts in the capital. The 16th century had seen Ottoman fortunes at their height, under Suleiman the Empire had achieved what later generations were to call a 'Golden Age' and Jews, to a great extent, had shared in it; had even been priveleged. With the death of Selim II in 1574, other nations began to assert their influence in the Court. The comparatively large communities of Greeks and Armenians had interests that in many ways ran counter to those of the Jews, these in turn were promoted through agents in close association or contact with the reigning Sultan. After the death of Ahmed I, his wife Kosem Mahpeyker Sultan, a Greek and no friend of the Jews, ruled almost supreme from the seclusion of the Imperial Harem between the years 1623 to 1651, when she was strangled. By the time of her death, Jews, Romaniot or Sephardic had not fared well in Constantinople. Subsequent to it, the following two Valides (Queen-mothers), Turhan and Rabia Gulnus, (the former a Circassian and the latter a Rethymniot) were responsible for dissipating the energies of the Empire and its people into that fatal malady that was earn it the title of The Sick Man of Europe.

Salonika, by contrast to Constantinoiple, had a quite different history. At the time of the Conquest it had been under-populated and the influx of Jews under Mehmet and Beyazid caused it to have a proportionately large Jewish presence that gave it a Spanish Jewish character. The harbor area was the main Jewish Quarter and it was sub-divided according to *Kehals* (small communities that were centred around synagogues), the names of which brought back memories of a Spain that was never to be seen again: Aragon, Castille, Saragossa, Toledo, etc. Jewish printing flourished in close association with houses in Constantinople and Amsterdam. The community was to a degree isolated and self-sufficient and this gave its inhabitants a more pronounced identity.

In other cities, such as Edirne and Izmir (Smyrna), this inner communal strength was not so readily apparent due to the large communities of Greeks, Armenians, and Turks within them, which kept the Jews numerically a minority. Nonetheless, the communities were strong and secure until they were suddenly faced with an inner crisis that shook every Jewish community in the Empire to its roots, and eventually caused divisions and apostasy that reached far into the West.

The roots of this crisis lay in the fact that after the period of adjustment began to provide security, speculations concerning the meaning of the exile from Spain began to excite the minds of mystics and rabbis. While it is true that the great center of Hispano-Jewish mysticism was to become Safed in Eretz, it was in the schools of Salonika that many Rabbis such as Joseph Caro, the mystic and author of the *Shulchan Aruch*, studied, taught, and sharpened their thought before moving on into Eretz. *Lehah Dodi*, the mystical hymn that Isaac Luria used to go into the fields singing to welcome the Sabbath, was written there by Solomon Alkabetz.

That mysticism and preoccupation with hidden

meanings and the fulfillment of prophecies, should become the main intellectual preoccupation of the rabbis of Salonika, Constantinople, and Eretz is not surprising. A similar interest in mysticism was characteristic of the last period of Romaniot religious creativity under the Palaeologues. In the face of imminent disaster, men's minds turned toward finding some deeper significance in the signs of the times. Romaniot mysticism had its own Kabbala that could trace its transmission back to the ancient schools of Palestine. The roots of Sephardic mysticism are more complicated, but after the 13th century it was mainly dependant on the Zohar or Book of Splendour. The Zohar incorporates the esoteric doctrines of Spanish Judaism as compiled by Moses Shem Tov de Leon. Much like the Jews of the Byzantine Empire those of Spain had, until the late 14th century, known little if any persecution. Whereas the Jews of Europe had been buffeted by wave after wave of violence since the Crusades, those of Spain had known security and had also risen high in the economic and commercial life of the Iberian Peninsula. With the Expulsion in 1492 there came a shock that was only explicable in the language of the Book of Lamentations written after the Fall of Jerusalem in the 6th century BCE. For many it was as significant an event as the destruction of the 2nd Temple in 71 CE, and the expulsion that occured after the failure of the Bar Kochba revolt, when the Jews were dispersed among the Nations. It was natural that men sought to find the significance of this new Exile; was it perhaps the beginning of the Ingathering that was to preceed the coming of the Messiah?

As if to reinforce the legitimacy of such musings, large numbers of Jews began to immigrate into Ottoman lands from Eastern Europe, especially from Poland where Jews had also lived almost priveleged lives for some time. With the Chmielnicki pogroms, Eastern European Jewry also found a haven in Ottoman territories as Jews of the remainder of Europe, living mainly in the Netherlands or Germany, looked on with concern. In 1648 a young Rabbi from Izmir announced that he was the Annointed One of God and was promptly banished from the city by its Jews. Rejected and exiled, Shabbetai Zvi took on himself the burden of the Messianic role. For the next fifteen years he attracted, through his songs, his beautiful voice, and his charisma, a large following of disciples, one of the most important of whom was a young mystic from Gaza called Nathan who confirmed that Shabbetai was the Messiah, and that he himself was Elias who was to go before him. Financially they were assisted by a wealthy Jew of Alexandria, Joseph Chelebi, and in 1662 Nathan sent out a circular letter to the communities of the Diaspora announcing that the Messianic Age would begin in 1666. In Jerusalem the news was met by the Jewish Community with an almost ecstatic hysteria. Shabbetai had been livng there for some time and as news spread to other communities the Jews became divided in their allegiance to, or rejection, of the Messiah. Some of the greatest rabbinical names of the time accepted him, such as Moses Galante and Samuel Primo. In Europe, as news reached communities there, excitement over the Messiah attracted funds, emigration, and even conversion to Judaism. Accounts circulated about strange miracles, even battles, and in Amsterdam several highly esteemed Portuguese rabbis including Moses D'Aquilar and Isaac Aboab, went over to him. It was not only mystics and fools who were attracted, however: Spinoza and one of his students, Dionysios Musaphia sent funds as well as messages. Salonika, the center of Jewish mystical thinking, was split and its synagogues became centers for debate. Finally, in 1666, not long after Shabbetai had mounted an ivory throne in Izmir, he was called to Constantinople and there received by the Sultan. There are many tales of miracles and of the pressures that were put on him during this time. He also was visited in seclusion by the Jewish physician to the Sultan, who was a convert to Islam. In the end, after a fortnight,Shabbetai himself accepted Islam and not long after was sent into Thrace with a new name, Aziz Mehmed Effendi. He died in 1676, after having prophesied the date of his death, with only a handful of followers about him, and leaving a serious legacy of division in almost every Jewish community in the Ottoman Empire and Europe. Not long after his death, many of his followers in Salonika went over into Islam. If the Messiah was to become all things in order to redeem them, then it was only natural that he had entered into the House of Darkness, i.e. mystical apostasy, as well. Shabbetai was *resurrected* in the minds of his followers and out of their conversion to Islam there emerged a new community in Salonika known as the Dönme, or converts. As Shabbetaeans they maintained close ties with their associates all over Europe where they were despised by Orthodox Jews who now repudiated all connection with the mystical schools of Judaism that they felt had nurtured Shabbetaism. Judaism tended as a consequence to become legalistic to an extreme and to be dominated by rabbis who had little sympathy with attempts to experience God other than by adherance to the Law. The central European Hassidim were in a sense an acceptable form of ecstatic Jewish sect—but the difficulties that it encountered with the Orthodox Jewish elite are well known and certainly rooted in the Shabbataean disaster.

The Dönme maintained their identity, though divided into four main sects, well into the 20th century. In 1927 they were forced to leave Salonika and find new homes in Turkey though they had made a request of the Beth Din of the city that they be considered Jews...in this way, by some twist of fate, they were saved the horrors of the Holocaust that virtually eradicated the Jews of Greece.

Other disasters followed on the heels of the internal crises of the Jews, especially in Salonika. In the early part of the century, five fires swept through the city destroying libraries and communal property. The Ottoman Empire was faced with economic crises as well as military losses that were the first signs of its final decline into lethargy. The Jews, completely identified with the Ottoman economy, began to suffer accordingly as the eyes of Europe turned from the East towards the Americas, and India or China by means of Africa. Radical change characterized Europe during this period of the Enlightenment and the Empire had no way of meeting the challenges other than by a radical reform for which it was ill-equiped. Reforming Sultans, such as Osman and Selim III were killed as soon as their intentions were discovered. When reform finally was achieved in one sphere,—the army—under Mahmoud II in the early 19th century, it was too late. By the time the Empire finally collapsed in the 20th centunry, the Jews had shared in all of its death agonies.

The number of Jews who lived at the turn of the 18th century in the territories that were eventually to become the Modern Greek State is unknown. The communities were complex, independant, and sharply defined as a consequence of differences in their contacts with external influences, and of the geography of Greece, dominated as it is by mountains and surrounded by seas. Broadly speaking Romaniot Jews were found mainly in the western parts of Greece, such as Epirus, where three very ancient communities existed at Ioannina, Arta, and Preveza. These were closely associated to the Jews of Kerkyra (Corfu), especially Arta and Preveza. Ioannina had a mixed community, some of its members being Sikiliotes, (having come from Sicily, quite possibly in the 13th century). The Jews of Corfu were under Venetian rule and had their own dialect—(called Pouliezi) indicating the origins of many from communities in Apuleia. The Jews of Zakynthos, also under Venice, maintained close associations with the Jews of Hania in Crete that dated back to before the Ottoman conquest of the island in the 17th century. The Jews of Crete had very ancient roots extending into the period before the Common Era. After the Venetian occupation, its communities received Jews from Venice, and to these newcomers were added others from North Africa and then Sephardic Jews who began to arrive early in the 15th century. The Jews of Rhodes were originally

Romaniot but after the conquest of the island by Suleiman in the 16th century, the community fell on bad times especially with the arrival of Sephardic settlers who were sent by the Sultan. The Gregos were completely absorbed and lost their identity though a synagogue under that name was retained until the 20th century. The Jews in the Aegean area adjacent to Rhodes also were Sephardic. The Peloponessos had many communities. All of them, such as Patras, Mistra, and Modon, being very ancient and mainly Romaniot, though a few names indicate that some were Ashkenazic and had probably been established in the 16th century or later. (The family of Shabbetai Zvi was originally from Patras and was of Ashkenazic background). Others were Sephardic. Halkis had a community that claimed to have been founded by none other than Alexander the Great when he sent back Jewish slaves from Judaea.

The east and central parts of mainland Greece were heavily Sephardic. 'Larissa had earned the name a Mother of Israel, and nearby Trikala was closely connected to it.. Salonika, Serres, Drama, Didi-moteicho, and Kavalla, were the great centers of the Sepharadim, well into the 20th century.

Entrenched as they were in Ottoman life, and tied economically to the fortunes of the Empire, these communities were caught in the midst of momentous events that were to destroy some and irrevocably change others.

In 1821 the Albano-Greeks in the Peloponessos broke out in rebellion much against the interests and wishes of the Phanariote Greeks (descendants of the old Byzantine aristocracy) in Constantinople. The response of the Porte was to execute the Patriarch, Gregory, and when news reached the insurgents that the executioners who killed him and those who subsequently threw his body in the Bosphoros were Jews, an open massacre of the Jews of the Peloponessos broke out. It is estimated that perhaps five thousand persons died or were forced to move north into Ottoman-held territories. Patras, Tripoli, Modon, Kalamata and Mistra, as well as Corinth, saw an end to Romaniot Jewish presence.

Following on the creation of the Greek Kingdom in 1834, the early modern Greek state set its eyes on recovering what it considered to be its historic lands. Greece was not alone in this. As if some giant hand had moved a kaleidescope, the component communities and minorities in the Balkans now suddenly assumed a new form. The Bulgarians, Serbs, Albanians, and one should not forget—the Turks themselves—now began to demand autonomy or freedom from the Ottomans and the creation of national states. By 1904 the Jews found themselves surrounded by new nations. Some of their co- religionists whether Romaniot or Sephardic were now assuming identities as Bulgarians, Serbs, etc. In 1912, after the Second Balkan War, Greece seized Salonika and absorbed into itself a city that was predominately Jewish, Spanish speaking and if not Ottoman in some of its sympathies, having a character decidedly its own. The city had already started becoming Europeanized much in the manner of Istanbul. Under Sabri Pasha, in the '90's of the 19th century, its old walls had been broken open and the city began to spread out beyond their limits. Broad boulevards were designed, new quarters and neighborhoods established and villas and large urban mansions erected in the contemporary taste of Europe. Its commercial connections were complex and its Jews were in close contact with similar Sephardic communities in Monastir, Sophia and Edirne, not to mention Istanbul. Overnight all of this changed.

There is no doubt that Salonika was a Jewish city in its heart. Over one-third of its population was Jewish, a proportion that does not include some twenty five thousand Donmes who considered themselves neither Jewish nor Turkish. The Christian community was not homogeneous and was made up of Bulgarians, Greeks, Serbs and Armenians. Commerical life came to a standstill on Friday evenings until the end of the Jewish Sabbath. The language of internal commerce was Ladino, and the heart of Salonika beat within the confines marked out by an enormous cemetary which held the remains of the ancestors of these Spanish Jews whose identity, at least to themselves, was no problem. Some thirty six synagogues were scattered within the Jewish Quarter still bearing names such as Moghrebi Catalan, etc. There were Jewish newspapers, cultural centers, several schools and many presses and hospitals, orphanages and homes for the aged. In short, Salonika was a Sephardic island in the midst of a troubled sea of nationalism.

For the Jews in the western Ottoman Empire, i.e. along the coast of the Aegean and the Balkans, these were very disturbing times, as Jewish identity was being called into question. Zionism had never been enthusiastically received among Jews in these areas, if only due to the fact that hitherto Palestine had lain within the confines of the Empire and was, in a sense, accessible. Jewish identity was also based not simply on religious grounds but had strong cultural roots that were the consequence of hundreds, if not at least a thousand, years of adaption. In Salonika the language and customs brought from the Iberian Peninsula four hundred years before easily replaced religious affiliation as an alternative identity for increasingly large numbers of secularized Jews. The Romaniot Jews were strongly Greek in their orientation and language as well as customs and traditions. By 1912, however, their communities were beginning to feel the consequences of regional nationalism.

The Jews of Athens were also in the process of developing a community. It would seem that its Jews had either fled or been massacred when the town (as it had been then) fell to the Greeks. With the arrival of King Otto there also came a number of advisors of Ashkenazic background and Jews from elsewhere, even Gibraltar, who tried in vain to create a small community. Jews were not popular, and it is not surprising to find that Athenian Jews did not take advantage even of a substantial legacy that had been left to them for the purpose of building a synagogue by the eccentric and Judaeophil Duchess of Plaissance. The Athenian Community only obtained a charter and formal recognition in the last decade of the 19th century, by which time many of its members were from Izmir, Chios, and other islands in the Aegean having been attracted to the capital for the same reasons as many Greek Christians.

In 1912, with the absorbtion of Salonika into the modern Greek state it was inevitable that things were to change. Salonika was a much larger city than was Athens. Its history, while not as prestigious, could be traced back to the 4th century BCE. Its Christian past was reflected in great monuments and churches that gave evidence of Imperial favour and a genuine urban tradition that Athens could not lay claim to. If Salonika was to become Hellenized according to the definitions characterizing all nationalisms in the 19th century, then the Jews were going to present a problem. It is not oversimplifying the picture to say that in general Romaniot Jews tended to look toward Athens and to assert their Greekness to a degree that was consistent with their history and traditions. Sephardic Jews, on the other hand, could not so easily relate to either Athens or Salonika if they lived in other communities. The Salonika Community was known for being a closed world, even to other Jews.

Wars, social upheaval, commercial crises and even crop failures prompted a wave of emigration from Greece of both Greek Jews as well as Christians. Between 1912 and 1920 there was a steady stream of emigration that saw the creation of large Greek Christian communities in the U.S. as well as smaller Jewish ones there and elsewhere. From Kastoria, Ioannina, Crete, and Salonika Jews made their way to Europe or the U.S. The Jews of Rhodes also began to leave the island in large numbers and several communities such as Chios and Kos ceased to exist at all due to emigration. The great fire of 1917 that destroyed almost all of the Jewish Quarter of Salonika aided in the movement of Jews into Athens or elsewhere. It also assisted in forcing the Jewish community to rebuild itself with an eye to a new era that was to be marked by Hellenism, the adoption of Greek language and cultural identity.

It can safely be said that the challenge was being met with some success by the late 1930's. The debris caused by the the events of the First World War and those of the Smyrna (Izmir) disaster, was settling. The attraction of the Mandate of Palestine was very limited to the Jews of Greece and Zionism took the form of investment rather than immigration. Jews were gradually becoming more deeply involved in the cultural, social and commercial life in Greece and anti-semitism was no real issue except in areas where jealousy and greed fanned it into flame. Salonika was the only place where it became especially virulent and this was the direct consequence of the settling of thousands of Greek refugees in the city during the 1927 exchange of populations between Greece and Turkey. The new arrivals were not necessarily Hellenists, they had lived comfortable enough lives in Turkey and had suddenly been uprooted from what had been their homes from ancient times, to be settled in a city that was completely foreign to them. Poor, desperate, frightened and little cared for after their arrival by the proper authorities, they became a natural breeding ground for a xenophobia that took the form of anti-semitism.

On October 28, 1940, an ultimatum was sent to the Greeks by Mussolini demanding immediate surrender to Italian forces that were gathered in the Albanian passes. The answer by Prime Minister Metaxas was a resounding *Oxi* (No), and Greece was thus drawn into the Second World War. Greeks were mobilized—Jews as well as Christians—and in a few months the Italians were driven back only to be rescued from complete humiliation by the arrival of the Germans. On April 6, 1941 the Germans invaded, and on April 21st they entered Athens and subsequently seized all of Greece and Crete.

The entire story of the almost total destruction of Greek Jewry has not been told nor will it be told here. In the face of doubts, revisionism, and perhaps the cynicism that we have developed in the course of experiencing or reading of the horrors of our industrialized century, it can only be said that in 1939 there were over seventy thousand Jews in Greece living in communities that had histories stretching back over two thousand years or whose family memories took them back into the rich brocade of Medieval Islamic Spain. In 1945, just after the end of the repatriations, the total Jewish presence in Greece was given as ten thousand. Those who had not returned had died in Poland. In some towns a few Jews either survived the deportations, emerged from hiding or survived even the camps; but they returned to find emptiness. Of the Jews of Crete none survived on the island and today the Jewish Quarter in Hania has only its empty synagogue, abandoned by Jew and Christian alike: there is not even a monument to com-memorate the tragedy. In Zakynthos all of the Jews were saved through the efforts of its Archbishop and Mayor; while on nearby Corfu the Mayor and Chief of Police declared a public holiday on the day in which the Jews were deported. From Salonika fifteen trainloads, departing over a period of eight months, were necessary to empty the city of its Jews. Today it is impossible to imagine what Malkha Israel (Salonika) must have been like when its Jews gave it a panache that one still senses in the midst of the present urban confusion. The Bulgarians, in the manner of Pilate, handed the five thousand Jews of Thrace to the Germans on the Danube. Their fates were sealed at Treblinka.

Only forty years have passed since then. The adjustment on the part of the Jews of Greece has been difficult, and understandably, slow. No family that survived was without a list of vanished relatives that could run into eighty or hundred persons. Some could

54

not bear the silence of old neighbourhoods, of the quarters and haunts that had drawn them back, the ghosts of which left only with difficulty. Still others seem to have been drawn back to these places precisely for these reasons: it was here that they were closest to their roots. Some emigrated, still others came to Athens, while a few remained in towns that will eventually absorb them and their decendants.

It has been said that the Jews of Greece are now vanishing. It has even been predicted that within twenty years there will be no Jews, only individuals living isolated and secularized lives. This remains to be seen. Unlike the Jewries of Europe, the Jewish presence in Greece is old— more than two thousand years—and with the exception of the Second World War there has never been a moment of unrelenting persecution. There have been times when they have all but vanished only to suddenly witness the rebirth of communities or the arrival of Jews from elsewhere, for the Jews of Greece have on more than one occasion offered haven to those fleeing from far-off lands thus adding to their own numbers. We are living in a time of quite momentous changes. The much criticised lack of Jewish religious leadership is neither unique to the Jews of Greece nor to Judaism; it is generally true in our secularist age. At the same time one can already see a breaking down of the naive belief our age has held that politics and politicians offer ideals and an integrating system of beliefs that would replace our inner-most spiritual needs. What will fill this vacuum? In Islamic nations the answer is a return to fundamentalism, and experience has shown that that is not a necessarily fruitful solution. Immigration to Israel has leveled off, at least in Greece and elsewhere in the Diaspora, and we are once again seeing a situation in which the Jews who live outside of Eretz find themselves perplexed and overwhelmed by issues beyond their abilities either to comprehend, or at times support, much less control. The revolt of Bar Kochba that led to the complete destruction of the Jewish homeland, has a side to it other than that symbolized by Masada ...

Greece will imminently enter the EEC. Its borders will be open in a manner that none of us can really appreciate. How this will effect both the Jews and Christians of Greece is only now being discussed, argued and questioned, as a concern regarding national identity as a whole. In the midst of such change it would be both rash and foolish to attempt to foresee its evolution and denouement.

Bibliographical note:

A great deal of research is being carried out on every aspect of Judaeo-Greek history. It is not within the scope of this essay to extend its length by the addition of a bibliography. Mention must be made, however, of three excellent publications that are both current as well as replete.

Attal, R.,   *Les Juifs de Grece - Bibliographie*,   Ben Tzvi Institute, Jerusalem,   1984.

Mor, M., & Rappaport, U.,
   Bibliography of the Works on Jewish History in the Hellenistic and Roman Periods / 1976- 1980. Zalman Shazar Centre, Jerusalem 1984.

Material in these two excellent bibliographies is added to and updated in the *Quarterly Bulletin of Judaeo-Greek Studies* edited by Prof. Nicholas de Lange and Ms. Judith Humphrey. The Quarterly contains all recent publications, monographs and articles on Judaeo-Greek History as well as notices regarding research projects and seminars. Subscription can be made to: The Bulletin of Judaeo-Greek Studies,
University of Cambridge,
Faculty of Oriental Studies
Sidgwick Avenue,
Cambridge CB3 9DA
UK

The Throne of Moses in the remains of the synagogue of Delos.

Josephus mentions the existence of a community on Delos in the 1st century CE. It is generally accepted by scholars today that this relatively small building was the synagogue and can be dated to the 1st century BCE, which makes it the oldest known synagogue in the Diaspora.

The Synagogue of Sardes (Sirt), c. 350 CE.

Sardes was known to have had a very large Jewish community, which is confirmed by the remains of its synagogue. In the course of excavations carried out in this century the sanctuary and forecourt revealed a quite enormous structure with two raised aedicules on the west in which were most likely kept the Torah scrolls. At its eastern end was a synthronos set in an apse that served the needs of the elders of the community. Before this was a marble table and almost central to the axis there is evidence of supports for a wooden structure that may have been the bema, or reader's desk.

Lintel stones from the synagogue of Corinth, 4-5th century CE.

The exact location of the synagogue of Corinth is un-known and to date only this fragment and part of an inscription have been found—though in different sections of the site of the ancient city. The most widely and commonly used Jewish symbol at this time was the Menorah accompanied by Lulav and Etrog, and similar symbols have been found both in Eretz as well as in Rome and elsewhere in Greece.

The synagogue of Athens in the Agora, 5th cent. CE.

This building is still debated over but its location, 'occidentation', apsidal recess and throne are characteristic of many Hellenistic synagogues. Not far from the site a small marble revetment bearing a Menorah and Lulav was found. Nothing is known of the Athenian Jews, and their presence in the city may well have been established quite late, as St. Paul in the Acts appears to address a gentile audience. This building was constructed in very insecure times as various invasions were occuring in Greece. In the late 4th century the Visigoths destroyed a great deal of Athens and it is most likely that the synagogue was built on an abandoned site at that time. In the following century other attacks forced the Athenians—Gentiles and Jews alike—to flee to the nearby island of Aegina where the Jews built a new synagogue, the mosaic floor of which can still be seen.

Byzantine Jews: Ms. Dionysiou 537, Mt. Athos, 10th century.

Jews appear frequently in Byzantine illustrations, ikons, and mosaics, and most probably they appear in contemporary dress. The heads of males are covered by a *soudarion* (head-scarf) and over their tunics they wear a very conservative and ancient garment known as a *paenula* which was cut in an oval or round form and thus avoided the corners that would have required *tsitsioth* (ritual fringes) required by the Mosaic Law.

An *Aleph* (wall amulet). Patras, 19th century.

Romaniot Jews had many customs that were slightly different from those of the Sepharadim. The *Aleph* was a kind of amulet with various Names of God written in mystical codes for the purpose of warding off the wiles of Lillith, the first wife of Adam. She was considered to be especially active during the fourty days after child-bearing when she attempted to smother both mother and child. *Alephot* were inscribed with the name of the child, the date of circumcision as well as the names of three especially powerful angels—Sanvai, Sansanvai and Samang-loph. It is of interest that such amulets were not prepared for female children, the birth of which was not generally celebrated.

יברכך ה' וישמרך יאר ה' פניו אליך ויחנך ישא ה' פניו אליך וישם לך שלום ׃

שמע ישראל ה' אלהינו ה' אחד בשכמל"ו ואהבת את ה' אלהיך בכל לבבך ובכל
נפשך ובכל מאדך והיו הדברים האלה אשר אנכי מצוך היום על לבבך ושננתם
לבניך ודברת בם בשבתך בביתך ובלכתך בדרך ובשכבך ובקומך וקשרתם לאות
על ידך והיו לטוטפת בין עיניך וכתבתם על מזוזת ביתך ובשעריך המלאך הגואל
אותי מכל רע יברך את הנערים ויקרא בהם שמי ושם אבותי אברהם ויצחק
וידגו לרוב בקרב הארץ יאבו כפי בפיע כציעש

כּוֹרֵךְ פֵּרוֹמֵי אִין מָצָּה מֵה שַׁד׳ טְרִיָא חַרְצָא קֵי טִי מָרוֹר פוּ
בָּצָרוֹ קֵי קוֹפְטוּמֵיקֵי דִינוֹמֵי קָתִי אִינוֹ אִישֵׁא קֵידִין אֵלִיס קֵי
עִין נָדְלִיגוֹמֵי מִי טוֹ חָרוֹר טוֹ בָּצָרוֹ קֵי פוֹ וּפַחְמִי סְטוֹ כָרוּסֵת
קֵי לֵמִי׳ מָצָּה וּמָרוֹר בְּלוֹ בְּרָכָה זֵכֶר לְמִקְדָּשׁ כְּהַלֵּל הַזָּקֵן שֶׁהָיָה בוֹרֵךְ
וְאוֹכְלָן בְּבַת אַחַת לְקַיֵּים מַה שֶׁנֶּאֱמַר עַל מַצּוֹת וּמְרוֹרִים יֹאכְלֻהוּ :
יִשְׁלָן עוֹרְף פּוּנְלָא אַרְדִינַחְסְנִי נָפָמִי אוֹמֵי מֵס אִירְדָט אוּ תַּיְאוּס
אֵפּוּן פֵרוֹמֵ׳ אִין תֵּי׳סֵי אִין מֵצָּה פוּ אֵיפִיקַמֵן אַפּוּקָטוּ טוּ טְרַפֵּזִי יָא
אֵפִיקוֹמִין קֵי דִינוֹ קֵי דִינוֹמֵ כֵּתִי אִינוֹ אִישֵׁא מֵי מֵיאָה אֵילָא קֵי
לֵמִי זֵכֶר לְקָרְבָּן פֶּסַח הַנֶּאֱכָל לְשׂוֹבַע :
בָּרַךְ זְמִיזוֹמֵה שַׁד׳ זֵ׳לָא קֵי לֵמֵי פוּ הַלֵּל : בִּרְכַּת הַמָּזוֹן
נִרְצָה לֵימֵיטוֹן בְּרָכָה אֱכָרוֹנָה קֵי אַסְטְפֵּרָא טוּ יְהִי רָצוֹן ק׳
הַלֵּל יִמִיזוֹמֵי פָּא זֵלָא קֵי לֵמֵי פוּ הַלֵּל :

Instructions for Seder written in Greek using the Hebrew
alphabet, Ioannina 20th century.

The Romaniot or Greek-speaking Jews maintained customs and traditions that indicate that their knowledge of
Hebrew was at times defective or even lacking. Justinian's
ordinance that Jews be required to hear the Torah read in the
Septuagint Greek on Shabbat was prompted by the fact that
Jews did not understand the scriptures in Hebrew, much less in
the Aramaic Targum. The Ioannina Jews in this and the last
century knew their Hebrew, so that this custom of writing out
texts in both languages reflects a tradition rather than a need.

Overleaf.

      Map showing the route taken through Byzantine territories in the 12th century by Benjamin of Tudela. The main source of information regarding displacement, occupations and the condition of Byzantine Jews rests on the account of travels made by this Jewish gem merchant of Tudela Spain. Benjamin arrived in Byzantine territory via Kerkyra in 1168 and followed an itinerary that took him through the main centres of Jewish life. His account provides an important insight not only into the condition of Byzantine Jews but also gives us a picture of Byzantine society as a whole as it was undergoing crucial changes just prior to the Fourth Crusade.

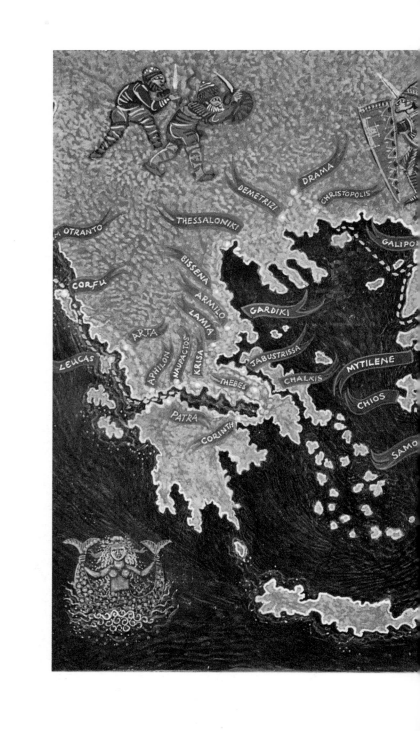

Sultan Beyazid II, (1481-1512). The British Library, London.

Beyazid was the son of Mehmet the Conqueror and grandfather of Suleiman the Magnificent. He continued his father's policy of resettling cities in the Empire and is credited with permitting the mass emigration of Sephardic Jews from Spain and Portugal into the haven of the Empire. It was with his permission that the first printing press was established in Constantinople (Istanbul) by David Ben Nahman, which saw the production of Jewish books in great numbers, and anticipating by threee hundred years the printing of books by either Muslims or Christians.

74

A Jewish doctor and merchant. 1574 CE. Anonymous.
Album of water-colours, Gennadios Library, Athens.

This album was executed by an unknown artist who had
close connections with the Imperial household or the Saray in
Istanbul. Jewish doctors served a number of the Sultans
(Mehmet II, Beyazid, as well as Suleiman). In some illustrations they are shown wearing high scarlet caps which may have
been an indication of their profession. It is also possible,
however, that that form of distinctive headdress was adopted by
Sephardic Jews and is here contrasted to the normal yellow
turban of the Romaniot Jews worn by the merchant.

Iudeus medicus.   *Iudæus.*

Two Jewish woman. 1574 CE. Anonymous.
Album of water-colours, Gennadios Library, Athens.

In the water-colour of the two Jewesses the one on the left wears a yellow headcovering as well as a *ferace* (dust coat) that would have been worn out-of-doors. The woman on the right, however, is dressed in European, perhaps even more accurately, Venetian dress. It is known that only one household of Jews in Istanbul was allowed to retain European dress and that was immediate entourage of Dona Grazia Mendes. Since this album contains many specifically identifiable portraits of personages in the court or court circles of Sultan Selim II, it is tempting to think that this is in fact a portrait of the great benefactress.

Colophon from a manuscript copy of the *Kelimat ha-Goyim* of Maestro Prophiat ha-Ephodi. The Jewish Museum of Greece, 1578 CE.

80

The lower section of the colophon indicates that it was copied out by the scribe Joseph S. Catalani in the house of Don Jose Mendes in Galata in the year 1578. This rare and unique ms. contains the Kelimat as well as six other anti-Christian polemical texts. (The Jewish Museum of Greece).

Kal Kadosh Shalom, Rhodes, 16th century.

This is the oldest surviving synagogue in Greece and was erected in the years following the Ottoman conquest of the island. The original Rhodian Jews were Romaniot and it appears that many chose to depart the island along with the Knights of St. John, though others remained and maintained a synagogue that was still in use until the last World War with the name of Los Gregos. Under Suleiman a great number of Sephardic Jews were settled in Rhodes and a foreign visitor mentions that the Jews constituted a majority of the urban population. Kal Kadosh Shalom was the first of several new synagogues built to accomodate its needs. The high, well-lit and well-aired building is divided internally by three transverse sets of arches resting on quite massive columns. Central to the east wall is a door that leads to a small courtyard and on either side of door are located two *Ehals* (for keeping the Torah Scrolls) that have been re-built since the Second World War in the manner of the surviving two *ehals* in the ancient synagogue of Sardes. The *Bema* (reader's desk) is a large structure located just off the center, to the west, and is in keeping with Sephardic usage in Greece and western Turkey.

82

The Rojo Quarter of Salonika, from Stewart & Reeves, *Antiquites*, 17th century.

The great Jewish Quarter of Salonika was divided into a number of minor neighborhoods each centerd around one of its thirty two synagogues. The only depiction that we have of the Jewish Quarter prior to the 19th century is in this etching of four Roman caryatids holding up an entablature in what was the ancient Roman Agora of the city. These gave their name to the short street that ran behind them known in Turkish as Süretler (the Idols) and among the Jews as Las Inkantadas (the Sirens). The caryatids were removed to the Louvre by the French in the 19th century though the street retained its name until the great fire of 1917, when the neighborhood houses were gutted. The house depicted in this picture is a modest one story adaption of a recognizeable Ottoman type with an open *sofa* off of which are located various domestic rooms.

The Synagogue of Verroia, 18th century.

     The Jews of Verroia were Sephardic and strongly con-
nected by marriage and commerce with those of Salonika.
They inhabited a *mahallası* (quarter) that survives almost
completely intact; though today empty of Jews since the Nazi
action of 1943. The synagogue of Verroia is quite small and
was enlarged in the 19th century by extending its south wall
and building an interior *mehitza* (women's section). An older
one was located to the south. The fabric of the building is cut
stone with floors resting on wooden beams and supports that
are bedded in a sharp decline. Its inner division reflects the
Sephardic rite with an *Ehal* on the east wall and a provision for
a *Bema* (which was not permanent) on the west wall and a finely
paneled and coffered ceiling over the center of the east-west
axis.

86

SALONIQUE. — Synagogue des Italiens.

Kal Yashan Italia, Salonika, l9th century on older foundations.

Ironically we have very few pictures of the interiors of the great synagogues of Salonika. From what is known they were spacious and richly decorated, and conformed, for the most

part, to the Sephardic rite in architectural lay-out. In this postcard photo of the Italian synagogue certain peculiarities are apparent especially in the arched *ehal* that resembles an Ottoman Muslim *mihrab* or prayer-niche. This, and all of the great synagogues of this genre were destroyed in the great fire of 1917.

Dönme boy, Salonika c. 1880. Private collection.

The followers of Shabetai Zvi in Salonika were divided into a number of sects: some more Jewish than Muslim, others more Muslim than Jewish. Of the latter, many were well integrated into contemporary Ottoman society both secular as well as religious. Many individuals were closely associated with dervish orders, especially the Mevlana and Bektashi both of which had inner or secret teachings that stressed the unity of religious experience, the love of God and abandonment of self. This young boy is dressed in the habit of a Mevlana *acem* (novice). It is unlikely that he was an initiate as children were not allowed to enter the Order. He wears a tall *sikke* on his head and under his full length *biniş* he is wearing the deeply pleated *tennure* that was worn especially during the whirling dances for which the Mevlana dervishes were famous. Conforming to Muslim law, Dönme children were normally circumcised at about the age of twelve and it was customary for them to be dressed in special garments. It is most likely that this is a circumcision picture and the child was dressed in a manner indicating his family's close association with the Order.

A scene in the Kasım Paşa Cemetary of İstanbul, coloured lithograph by A. Preziosi, c. 1841.

Kasım Paşa cemetary still exists on the Galata side of the Halıc (Golden Horn). While this picture is geographically accurate (one can make out the minarets of the Mosque of Suleiman as well as the Tower of Beyazid), and the costumes correct, it is likely that the picture was composed rather than taken directly from life. The tomb against which the woman is resting is recognizeably 16th century. She is wearing a *makrama* (scarf), on her head. Muslim women would have worn a *yaşmak* (face ceil) made of two sections of muslin. Her *ferace* is distinctly Jewish insofar as it has a heavily decorated panel hanging down the back. The Rabbi, raggedly dressed and slovenly in appearance contrasts strongly with the sloe-eyed lady looking out of the picture and reflects Preziosi's fascination with Jewish ladies in general and distaste for Jewish men.

92

Family picture, Salonika, 1904.

Shortly before the turn of the 19th century Salonika underwent a radical urban development reflecting the efforts of the Ottomans to modernize the Empire. The Jews in the city very quickly took advantage of these changes and the new atmosphere and adopted European fashions—-and affectations—-that at times jarred with the religious community. This picture of the Benveniste family was undoubtedly taken in the garden of their home. All of the males and the young women are dressed in European fashions, whereas the mother is posing in the traditional dress of a Salonika Jewess.

Post-nuptial picture taken in the Jewish Quarter of Ioannina, 1904.

The Jewish Quarter of Ioannina was divided into two sections. One was located in what was called the Kastro, within the ancient city walls and had as its center the Kal Kadosh Yashan, (Old Synagogue) which still stands. As Ioannina expanded out of its city walls in the course of the 19th century the Jews also established a new quarter which was located along a street that is now named after Joseph Eliya, a local Jewish poet. On it, was built another synagogue, the Kal Kadosh Hadash, which was destroyed in the Second World War. This picture was taken in the new quarter just a few years before Ioannina was joined to Greece and shows an enormous crowd of Jews who had attended the wedding of a prominent Jew of the city. The bride is wearing European wedding dress and her mother is conservatively dressed as are most of the men who wear the fez to indicate that they are subjects of the Sultan.

Kal Kadosh Yashan, Ioannina, early 19th century.

This very grand synagogue was constructed in the early part of the 19th century and was located in the Kastro, or old town of Ioannina. Attatched to it was a small oratory known as the *minyan* as it was there that weekday prayers were normally fulfilled by the older men of the community. The synagogue proper is built as a square divided internally by eight columns with connecting arches. Midway along its central east-west axis, an inscribed dome set on pendentives marks the centre of the structure. At the eastern end of this axis is set a large neo-classic *ehal* and opposite to it, on the western end, is a grandly elevated *bema* set in an apse. The *mehitza* (women's section) is located in a balcony that runs the length of the building along its northern side. The main entrance to the synagogue is located on the west side. The liturgical peculiarities of Judaism dictate that prayers be directed toward the east (Jerusalem) but that honour be given to the Scrolls of the Law when they are moved out of the *Ehal* and taken to the *Bema* to be read. In other words a shift in direction is characteristic of certain parts of the liturgy. This traditional Romaniot schema provides ample space for such movement. The seating arrangement is such that divan-like benches are set parallel to the central axis. Persons sitting along it face each other, whereas others would have been seated back to back in parallel aisles to the north and south. This arrangement of the interior of a synagogue conforms to a system that was in general usage among Romaniot Jews and was influenced, to some degree by Venetian models; though, in the case of Ioannina, there may well be older and more local traditions at work.

R. E. Cohen, Athens, 1894.

In the same year that this picture was taken, the Athens Community was recognized as a legal entity under Greek law. Its original members had been mostly of Ashkenazic background, having arrived at the time of the establishment of the Kingdom. Prior to that time it is unlikely that there were any Jews and it was only with great difficulty that their numbers increased to such a degree that they could request legal recognition. By the end of the 19th century many Jews began to settle in Athens attracted by the settled conditions and other benefits. There were a good number from Ioannina, the Aegean Islands, as well as Asia Minor. R. Cohen was from Izmir (Smyrna) and one of the founders of the Community. Over his Western suit he is wearing a blue silk kaftan lined with fur and on his head a fez. Neither of these represent rabbinical dress of the time, though they clearly indicate his Anatolian origins.

Scene in the Jewish Quarter, Salonika, circa 1912/3.

A well-known sight in Salonika were the *hamals* (porters and stevedors) who worked the harbor areas. Almost all of them were Jews and they had a monopoly on the handling of goods. The young man in this picture is most likely working the harbour area near Freedom Square and next to him is a typical vendor of drinks who mostly was also Jewish. Such vendors were ubiquitous and their beverages changed with the seasons: apricot, cherry and plum in the spring and summer months replaced by cinnamon and mastic-laced hot *sahlep* in the winter. The soldier on the left is most likely a Bulgarian. (Note: There was a large emigration of some three thousand Saloniki *hamals* to Eretz, viz. Haifa, in the early 1930's.)

102

Overleaf.

Family picture, Hania, Crete, c. 1900.

Crete had a very ancient Jewish community that had dwindled considerably by the end of the 19th century. At the time when this picture was taken the majority of Jews the Jews of Crete lived in Hania, in an area known as the Ovraiki which had two synagogues. Crete was going through quite peculiar changes at the time, as the Ottomans formally left in 1896, and the island under a Greek regent was independant with its own parliament, customs, post etc. This status lasted until 1913 when Crete was annexed to the Greek mainland. During these and the following years there was a steady emigration of Cretan Jews so that by 1941 there were only three hundred seventy six remaining, and these mostly in Hania. This picture was taken in the garden of a Jewish family. The old gentleman in the center is wearing a fez and the women have their heads uncovered, as do the other men, which is an indication of contemporary assimilation.

Scenes in the Jewish Cemetary of Salonika, 1918.

The Jewish cemetary of Salonika was enormous and, as the city expanded beyond the ancient walls in the late 19th and early 20th centuries it was increasingly a problem. Visits to it were frequent and it was as much a place for socializing among the living as it was a place of repose for the dead. Scattered about were graves of relatives, friends and also revered rabbis whose intercession was greatly sought after. Mingling with visitors were professional prayer-readers known as *hanaci* who could be hired to recite necessary commemorations or perform other graveside tasks. This, and the following photograph, were taken in 1918, just a year after the great fire that destroyed a

large portion of the Jewish Quarter of the city. The two women
are dressed in the traditional Jewish costume. On the left the
woman is wearing on her head a *kofya* which was a confection
made up of a number of specially cut textiles the most striking of
which was a long snood of green brocade that hung down the
back. On its extremity was sewn a patch of velvet richly
embroidered with gold thread and seed pearls known as a *pudya*.
The short jacket lined with cat or rabbit fur was known as a
kapetana and under that, as can be seen in the case of the woman
on the right, was worn a long kaftan or *entari* over a wrap-
around skirt or *sayo*. Over the front of the *sayo* would have been
worn a *devantal* (long apron). The woman on the right has
folded a *kapetana* and is wearing it on her head as a sunshade.

Rabbinical official in the Jewish Cemetary of Salonika. 1918.
Rabbinical dress varied according to rank and also affiliation to
particular synagogues in the city.

In general rabbis wore a costume not unlike that of
mullahs (Muslim clerics), consisting of a striped kaftan and over
that a large *biniş* (outer coat-like garment). The turbans
indicated special functions. In the background can be seen the
cemetary stretching toward the city walls. This entire area was
bulldozed down during th German Occupation and today the
University of Salonika is built over it.

Purim celebration play, Larissa, 1918.

Purim in Greece was enthusiastically celebrated in every Jewish community. The *megillah*, relating the story of Queen Esther, was read in the synagogues to the accompaniment of much rowdiness at every mention of the name of the wicked Haman, and quite elaborate social events took place as well. Most the latter were in the form of Purim plays. Larissa was famous for these, perhaps a reflection of its title among the Sepharadim of Greece as a *Madre d'Israel* a title that was used as well for Queen Esther. The players here are dressed in a rich assortment of household embroideries and textiles many of them consisting of wrappers, towels, runners and even, in the case of Haman (to the left of Queen Esther), a velvet bridal dress.

El Puntchon, a satyrical newspaper of Salonika, 1925.

Salonika was traditionally famous for its printing, though, by the end of the 19th century it was being surpassed by the presses of Constantinople and Livorgno. It had several newspapers some of them religious in orientation and quite a few avant garde insofar as they represented political views of a secular nature. *El Puntcho* (the Pin Prick) was one of the most famous. It was written in Ladino using Rashi script and appeared weekly.

פריסייו 1 דראחמי ⁣ ⁣ ⁣ 1 מאיו 1925 ⁣ ⁣ לונס 7 מאיו 5685

EL POUNTSON
Εβδομαδιαία
Σατιρική
Εφημερίς
Οδός Σαλαμίνος, 1
Θεσσαλονίκη

EL POUNTCHON
Satirique
Hebdomadaire
1, Rue Salamine
Salonique

Qui bene amat bene castigat

F. D. L. M.

סאלוד אה טי או פרימאבירה

ייה סאלבימוס

קאליפ'ס פארה מוחיריס פ'אם

דולסי אי סאלאדו

טורה בי דדראר

מאטס די באד

Two ladies from Komotini. 1925.

Komotini was a Sephardic community and maintained close connections with other communities in Thrace. Prior to 1913 the town had a very complex population of Spanish speaking Jews, Turks, Pomoks, and Bulgarians, and it tended to associate itself more closely with Edirne than Salonika. The two women shown in this picture are wearing the traditional costume. The mother, to the left, was Mrs Buena Tabah and her dark clothes indicate that she was a widow. Her daughter in-law Paulina| is wearing a typical velvet gold-embroidered jacket and gilt-edged apron.

The Trikala Synagogue, 1930.

Trikala is located not far from Larissa and was traditionally Spanish speaking, though a large number of the members of its Jewish community were Romaniot and maintained close ties with Ioannina. The synagogue is Sephardic in lay-out and is characteristic of a number of stark and unimaginitive buildings that were put up during these years.

116

The deportation of Jews from Kavalla in March 1943 by the
Bulgarians.

The Bulgarians were awarded certain parts of Macedonia
and Thrace as their share of the spoils of the conquest of Greece.
As they set their eyes on the *Bulgarization* of these territories, as
part of their dream of expanding into areas they considered to
be territorially their own, they took measures to terrify the
Christian population into flight. The Jews, as Greek citizens,
were singled out for special treatment. After severe curfews and
restriction of movement, they were finally rounded up in March
1943, gathered together at Kavalla, and then sent to Lom on the
Danube where they were passed over to the Germans. Little is
known of their fate after this, other than that they travelled by
boat up the Danube to Vienna and from there were sent to
Treblinka.

118

Overleaf.

The order of General Stroop putting into effect the Nurenberg Laws in the German Occupied zone of southern Greece, Athens 4.x.43 and Corfu 20.xi.43.

This order first appeared in Athens on the eve of Yom Kippour in 1943, just after the collapse of the Italians who had, as members of the Axis Alliance, held southern Greece as well as the Ionian and Dodecanese Islands, and Epirus. The Italians had been unwilling accomplices in the anti-semitic actions of the Germans and had not taken part in the mass deportation of the Jews from Macedonia and Thrace. This order was accompanied by notices in all of the newspapers of Greece and it clearly describes restrictions that were to be imposed on Jews including a curfew, and punishments that were to be meted out to Christians who assisted Jews. The last provision carefully defines a Jew as being a person who has three Jewish grand-parents, regardless of his religion. The mass arrest of the Jews occurred on 23 March, 1944 by which time they had been completely severed from normal society, or—-as in the case of many—-had either fled Greece or gone into hiding.

ANORDNUNG

1) Alle Juden im Befehlsbereich haben sich unverzüglich in ihren ständi[gen] Wohnsitz, den sie am 1.6.1943 bewohnten, zu begeben.

2) Es ist den Juden verboten, ihren ständigen Wohnsitz zu verlassen o[der] die Wohnug zu wechseln.

3) Die Juden in Athen und Vororten sind verpflichtet, sich binnen 5 [Ta]gen bei der Jüdischen Kultusgemeinde in Athen zu melden und sich dort [re]gistrieren zu lassen. Bei der Registrierung ist die ständige Wohnung anzugeb[en]. Ausserhalb Athens hat die Meldung bei den zuständigen griechischen Bür[ger]meister—oder Gemeindeämtern zu erfolgen.

4) Juden, die diesen Anordnungen nicht nachkommen, werden erschos[sen]. Nicht Juden, die Juden versteckt halten, ihnen Unterschlupf gewähren oder ih[nen] zur Flucht behilflich sind, werden in Arbeitslager eingewiesen, falls keine sch[we]rere Bestrafung erfolgt.

5) Juden ausländischer Staatsangehörigkeit haben sich am 15.11. 1943 08.00 Uhr bei der Jüdischen Kultusgemeinde in Athen einzufinden und dort unter Vorlage ihrer Staatsangehörigkeitsnachweise registrieren zu las[sen]. Ausserhalb Athens hat die Meldung bei den oben angeführten griechischen [Beh]örden zu erfolgen.

7) Die Jüdische Kultusgemeinde in Athen wird mit sofortiger Wirkung [zur] alleinigen Interessenvertretung aller Juden in Griechenland bestimmt. Sie hat un[ver]züglich einen Ældestenrat zu bilden und ihre Tätigkeit aufzunehmen. Weitere [An]weisungen ergehen zu gegebener Zeit.

7) Nach erfolgter Registrierung haben alle männlichen Juden vom vo[llen]deten 14. Lebensjahre ab sich jeden zweiten Tag bei den oben angeführten [Stel]len zu melden

8) Es ist den Juden verboten, Strassen und öffentliche Plätze in der [Zeit] von 17,00 Uhr bis 07,00 Uhr zu betreten.

9) Die griechischen Polizeibehörden werden angewiesen, die Durchfüh[rung] obiger Anordung auf das schärfste zu kontrollieren und zuwiderhandelnde J[uden] oder Personen, die ihnen bei der Nichtbeachtung der Anordung behilflich [sind] sofort feszunehmen.

10) Als Jude im Sinne dieser Anordung gilt, wer von mindestens drei [der] Rasse nach jüdischen Grosseltern abstammt, ohne Rücksicht auf die derze[itige] Religionszugegörigkeit.

Korfu 20-11-1943

Athen, den 4.10.1943

Der Höhere SS — und Polizeiführer
Griechenland

gez. **STROOP**

SS — Brigadeführer und Generalmajor
der Polizei

[signature]
Hauptmann

Feldkommandantur 1032

ΔΙΑΤΑΓΗ

1) Ἅπαντες οἱ εἰς τὴν περιοχὴν Γερμανικῆς Διοικήσεως εὑρισκόμενοι Ἑβραῖοι ὀφείλουν νὰ μεταβοῦν ἀνυπερθέτως εἰς τὰς μονίμους κατοικίας των, ὅπου παρέμενον τὴν 1—6—1943.

2) Ἀπαγορεύεται εἰς τοὺς Ἑβραίους νὰ ἐγκαταλείπουν τὴν μόνιμον κατοικίαν ἢ νὰ ἀλλάσσουν κατοικίαν.

3) Οἱ εἰς τὰς Ἀθήνας καὶ τὰ προάστεια εὑρισκόμενοι Ἑβραῖοι ὑποχρεοῦνται ὡς προσερχόμενοι ἐντὸς 5 ἡμερῶν εἰς τὴν ἑβραϊκὴν θρησκευτικὴν κοινότητα Ἀθηνῶν, ἐγγράφουν εἰς τὰ ἐκεῖ μητρῶα. Κατὰ τὴν ἐγγραφὴν ὀφείλουν νὰ δηλώσουν τὴν μόνιμον κατοικίαν των. Εἰς τὰς ἐκτὸς τῶν Ἀθηνῶν περιοχὰς ἡ δήλωσις πρέπει νὰ διενεργηθῇ εἰς τὰ ἁρμόδια ἑλληνικὰ δημοτικὰ ἢ κοινοτικὰ γραφεῖα.

4) Ἑβραῖοι, μὴ συμμορφούμενοι πρὸς τὰς διαταγὰς ταύτας, θὰ τυφεκίζωνται. Μὴ Ἑβραῖοι, οἱ ὁποῖοι ἀποκρύπτουν Ἑβραίους, παρέχουν αὐτοῖς καταφύγιον ἢ βοηθοῦν τούς, ὅπως δραπετεύσουν, θὰ μεταφέρωνται εἰς στρατόπεδα συγκεντρώσεως ἐφ' ὅσον δὲν ἐπιβάλλεται εἰς αὐτοὺς ἔτι βαρυτέρα ποινή.

5) Οἱ ξένης ὑπηκοότητος Ἑβραῖοι ὀφείλουν νὰ παρουσιασθοῦν τὴν **25-10**-43 καὶ ὥραν 8ην εἰς τὴν ἑβραϊκὴν θρησκευτικὴν κοινότητα Ἀθηνῶν καὶ ἐγγράφουν ἐκεῖ, ὑποβάλλοντες τὰ πιστοποιητικὰ τῆς ὑπηκοότητός των. Ἐκτὸς τῶν Ἀθηνῶν ἡ δήλωσις θὰ γίνεται πρὸς τὰς ἀνωτέρω μνημονευομένας ἑλληνικὰς ἀρχάς.

6) Ἡ ἑβραϊκὴ θρησκευτικὴ κοινότης Ἀθηνῶν ὁρίζεται, μὲ ἄμεσον ἰσχύν, ὡς νόμιμη ἀντιπρόσωπος τῶν συμφερόντων ὅλων τῶν ἐν Ἑλλάδι Ἑβραίων. Αὕτη ὀφείλει νὰ καταρτίσῃ ἄνευ ἀναβολῆς συμβούλιον γερόντων καὶ νὰ ἐπιληφθῇ τῆς ὀργανώσεώς της. Περαιτέρω ὁδηγίαι δοθήσονται ἐν δέοντι χρόνῳ.

7) Μετὰ τὴν ἐγγραφὴν ἅπαντες οἱ ὑπερβαίνοντες τὸ 14ον ἔτος τῆς ἡλικίας των ἄρρενες Ἑβραῖοι ὀφείλουν νὰ παρουσιάζωνται ἡμέραν παρ' ἡμέραν εἰς τὰς ἄνω ἀναφερομένας ὑπηρεσίας.

8) Ἀπαγορεύεται εἰς τοὺς Ἑβραίους νὰ διέρχωνται ἀπὸ τὰς ὁδοὺς καὶ τὰς δημοσίας πλατείας ἀπὸ τῆς 17.00 μέχρι τῆς 07.00 ὥρας.

9) Ἐφιστᾶται ἡ προσοχὴ τῶν ἑλληνικῶν ἀστυνομικῶν ἀρχῶν ὅπως ἐλέγχουν αὐστηρότατα τὴν ἐκτέλεσιν τῆς ἄνω διαταγῆς καὶ συλλαμβάνουν πάραυτα τοὺς παραβαίνοντας αὐτὴν Ἑβραίους ἢ τὰ πρόσωπα ἐκεῖνα τὰ ὁποῖα ὑποβοηθοῦν αὐτοὺς ὅπως παραβοῦν τὴν διαταγὴν αὐτήν.

10) Ἑβραῖος ὑπὸ τὴν ἔννοιαν τῆς διαταγῆς ταύτης θεωρεῖται πᾶς ὅστις κατάγεται ἐκ τριῶν τοὐλάχιστον Ἑβραίων τὴν φυλὴν προπατόρων, χωρὶς ἐν προκειμένῳ νὰ λαμβάνεται ὑπ' ὄψιν τὸ θρήσκευμα, εἰς τὸ ὁποῖον οὗτος ἀνήκει νῦν.

Ἐν Ἀθήναις τῇ 4 Ὀκτωβρίου 1943   *Κέρκυρα 20-11-194*

Ὁ Ἀνώτατος Ἀρχηγὸς τῶν Ταγμάτων Ἀσφαλείας
καὶ τῆς Ἀστυνομίας Ἑλλάδος
(ὑπογρ.) **ΣΤΡΟΟΠ**
Διοικητὴς Ταξιαρχίας Ταγμάτων Ἀσφαλείας
καὶ ὑποστράτηγος τῆς Ἀστυνομίας

The synagogue of Didimothichon, 20th cent.

This community, located as it was along the Turkish border, was considered to be in the German Occupied zone. Sephardic in minhag and traditions, it had traditional close ties with Edirne, Istanbul and Sophia. After the debris of the Balkan War (1913) and the First World War had settled, it began to enter a period of posperity. A new synagogue, school, and communal center were built in the 1930's. On the 8th of April, 1943, the entire community of nine hundred seventy persons was arrested by the Germans and eventually they were sent by rail to Auschwitz. The synagogue was of the Sephardic plan. Under the bay formed by the columns and arches would have been the bema. The building was savagely desecrated and left derelict. This picture was taken in 1984. Since then due to structural weaknesses, the building has been razed.

The restored synagogue of Patras in the Jewish Museum of Greece, 20th century.

During Medieval times the old community was mentioned frequently and it was obliterated during the Greek uprising against the Ottomans. Toward the end of the 19th century a sufficient number of Jews had established themselves to warrant creating a new community. Most of the new members were from Kerkyra (Corfu), Preveza, and Arta. In 1922 a small synagogue, school, and lodgings for a resident rabbi were built. Following the Venetian tradition, by way of Kerkyra, the synagogue proper was built on the first floor over the rabbi's lodging and common rooms that were located on the ground flooe. The lay-out was axially disposed with the *ehal* projecting from the eastern wall and the *bema* facing it from the western wall under an inscribed dome. Around the southern and northern walls were built seats and the centre aisle was formed by several rows of high-backed benches that faced each other running parallel to it. This polar-axial plan is typical of Romaniot synagogues in Greece. During the Occupation most of the community was arrested and the synagogue, quite remarkably, was sealed and not pillaged. At the termination of hostilities attempts were made to re-vivify the community. These ultimately failed and in 1979 the community was formally dissolved. Not long after, it was decided that the building be razed and the Jewish Museum was fortunate in being able to remove the most important parts of the interior as well as the contents of the *genizeh* (a special area set aside for storing damaged, or unwanted religious books, documents, and artifacts ultimately destined to be buried). In this were found many marriage contracts, amulets and some religious artifacts, that confirm the close associations that were maintained between Patras, Kerkyra, and Crete. On being reconstructed in the Jewish Museum of Greece, the synagogue was re-dedicated with the name *Ha Kabetz* by the Chief Rabbi of France, R. Samuel Sirat, on 29th April, 1984 when the Museum was formally inaugurated.

124

Photographic credits:

P. 75. The British Library, London.

Pp. 65, 69, 72-73, 83, 85, 87, 88-89, 91, 93, 95, 97, 99, 101, 102, 104-105, 106, 107, 109, 111, 115, 117, 118, 120-121, 123, 125. T. DeVinney.

P. 59. Dr. B. Goldfarb.

Pp. 77, 79. The Gennadios Library, Athens, Greece.

P. 61. N. Stavroulakis.

P. 63. Prof. C. Williams, Corinth Excavation.